PRIMARY MATHEMATICS 3A

WORKBOOK Part One

Third Edition

Primary Mathematics Project Team

Project Director
Dr Kho Tek Hong

Team Members
Chee Kum Hoong, Hector
Chip Wai Lung
Liang Hin Hoon
Lim Eng Tann
Lim Hui Cheng, Rosalind
Ng Hwee Wan
Ng Siew Lee

Curriculum Specialists
Cheong Ngan Peng, Christina
Ho Juan Beng
Sin Kwai Meng

CURRICULUM PLANNING & DEVELOPMENT DIVISION
MINISTRY OF EDUCATION, SINGAPORE

Marshall Cavendish Education

© 1982, 1992 Curriculum Development Institute of Singapore
© 1997, 1999 Curriculum Planning & Development Division
Ministry of Education, Singapore

Published by Marshall Cavendish Education
A member of Times Publishing Limited
Times Centre, 1 New Industrial Road, Singapore 536196
Customer Service Hotline: (65) 6213 9106
E-mail: fps@sg.marshallcavendish.com
Website: www.marshallcavendish.com/education/sg

First published 1982
Second Edition 1992
Third Edition 1999
Reprinted 1999, 2000 (twice), 2004 (twice), 2007

All rights reserved. No part of this publication may be reproduced, stored in a retrieval system or transmitted, in any form or by any means, electronic, mechanical, photocopying, recording or otherwise, without the prior permission of the copyright owner.

ISBN 978-981-01-5654-1

Illustrated by: Goh Ker Foo, Jesryn Pang

Printed in Singapore by Fabulous Printers Pte Ltd

ACKNOWLEDGEMENTS

The project team would like to record their thanks to the following:

- members of the Primary Mathematics Team who developed the first edition and second edition of the package
- members of the Steering Committee for the second edition of the package
- teachers who tested the materials in the package and provided useful insights and suggestions
- Educational Technology Division, for the design and production of the audio-visual components of the package
- all those who have helped in one way or another in the development and production of the package

CONTENTS

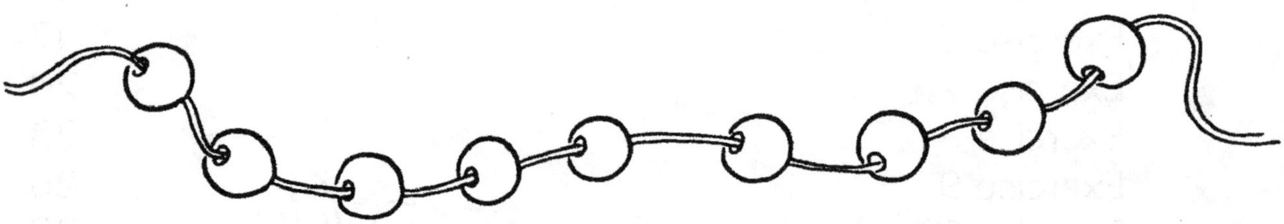

4×3
3×4

EXERCISE 1

1. Write the numbers.

(a)

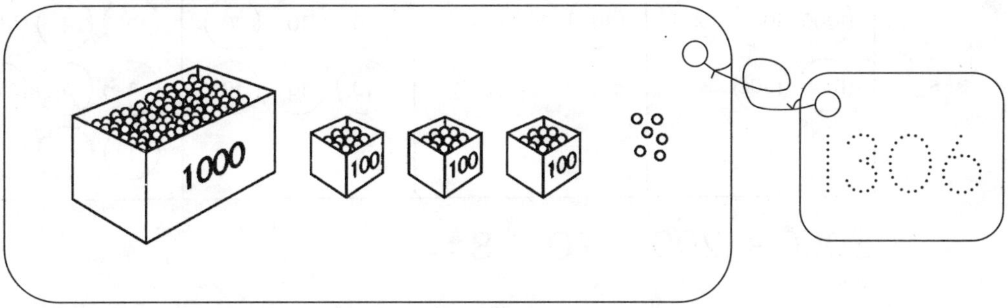

(b)

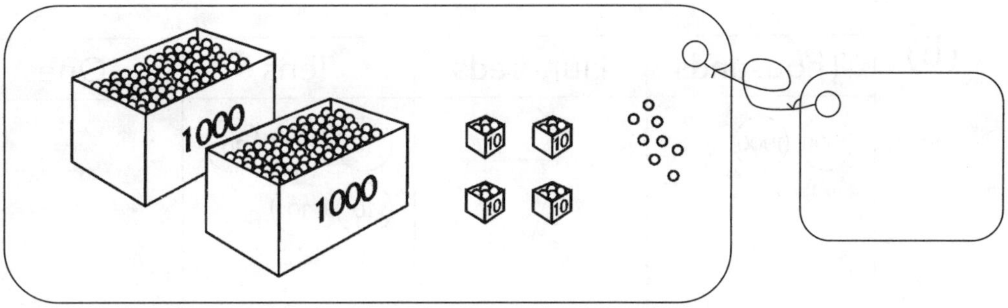

(c)

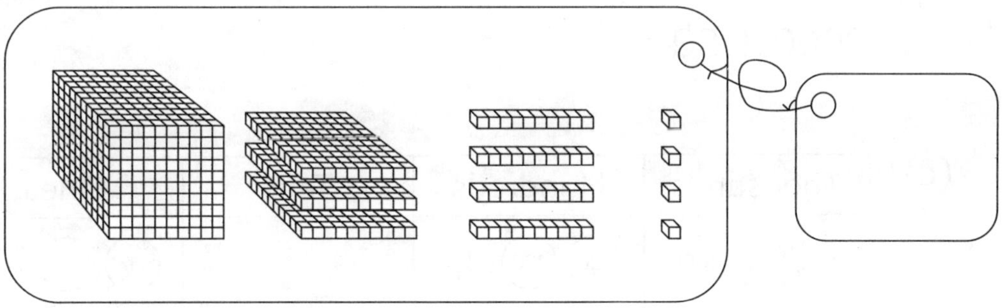

(d)

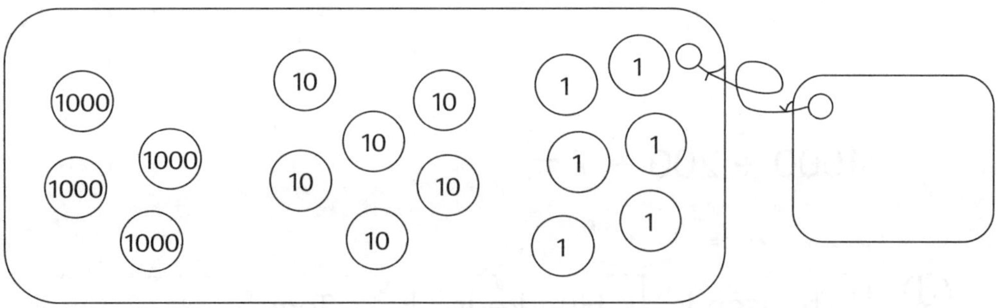

(e)

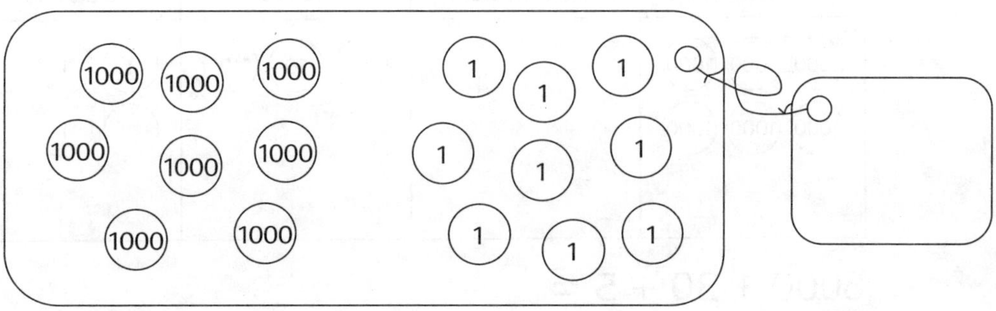

2. Write the numbers.

(a)

Thousands	Hundreds	Tens	Ones
1000 1000 1000 1000 1000	100 100	10 10 10 10 10 10 10	1 1 1 1 1 1 1 1

5000 + 200 + 70 + 8 =

(b)

Thousands	Hundreds	Tens	Ones
1000 1000		10 10 10 10 10	

2000 + 50 =

(c)

Thousands	Hundreds	Tens	Ones
1000 1000 1000 1000	100 100		1 1 1 1 1 1 1

4000 + 200 + 7 =

(d)

Thousands	Hundreds	Tens	Ones
1000 1000 1000 1000 1000 1000		10 10 10	1 1 1 1 1

6000 + 30 + 5 =

3. Fill in the blanks.

Thousands	Hundreds	Tens	Ones
5	**8**	**9**	**7**

(a) 5897 is a 4-digit number.

It is made up of __________ thousands,

__________ hundreds, __________ tens and

__________ ones.

(b) In 5897, the digit **5** stands for __________.

(c) In 5897, the digit __________ is in the **hundreds place**.

The value of the digit is __________.

(d) In 5897, the digit in the **tens place** is __________ and the digit in the **thousands place** is __________.

4. Fill in the blanks.

(a) In 3**8**01, the digit **8** stands for __________.

(b) In 7604, the digit __________ is in the **hundreds place**.

(c) In 52**6**3, the value of the digit 6 is __________.

(d) In 35**0**7, the digit **0** is in the __________ place.

(e) In 3895, the digit in the **ones place** is __________ and the digit in the **hundreds place** is __________.

EXERCISE 3

1. (a) Which is greater 4037 or 4073? ________

   (b) Which is smaller 5001 or 5010? ________

2. 3747, 4082, 3761, 3671

   (a) Which is the greatest number? ________

   (b) Which is the smallest number? ________

3. Fill in the blanks with the words **greater** or **smaller**.

   (a) 7685 is ________ than 7865.

   (b) 5025 is ________ than 5031.

   (c) 5203 is ________ than 5199.

4. (a) Arrange the numbers in order.
   Begin with the greatest.

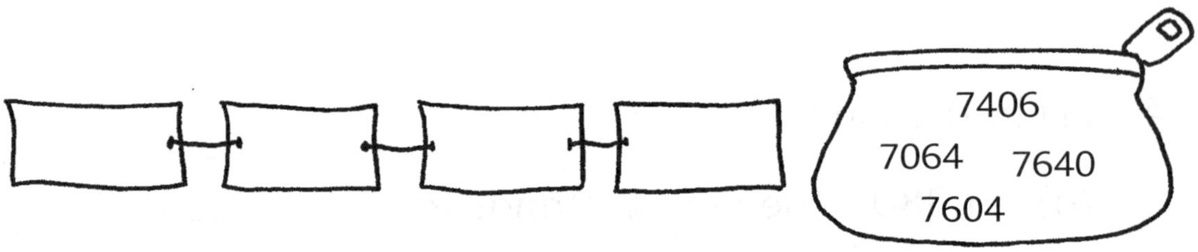

   (b) Arrange the numbers in order.
   Begin with the smallest.

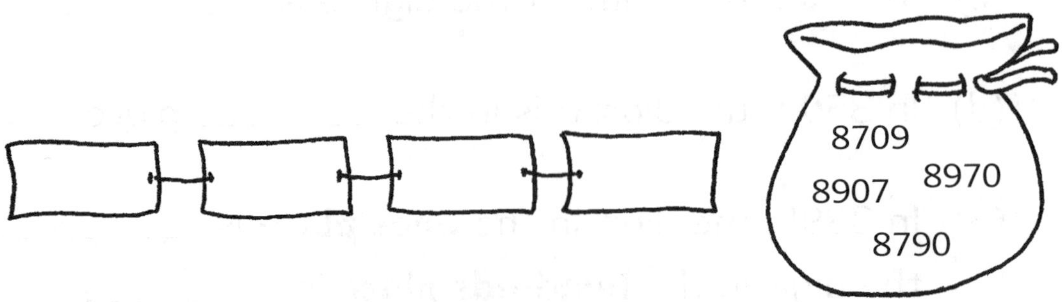

5. (a) Use these cards to make different 3-digit numbers.

The 3-digit numbers are:

(b) Use these cards to make different 3-digit numbers.

The greatest number is ________.

The smallest number is ________.

6. What is the greatest 4-digit number that you can make using all the digits 1, 0, 3, 8 ?

____

7. What is the smallest 4-digit number that you can make using all the digits 7, 5, 2, 6?

____

EXERCISE 4

1. Fill in the blanks.

(a)

Thousands	Hundreds	Tens	Ones
1000 1000 1000 1000 1000 1000	100 100	10 10 10	1 1 1 1 1

100

_________ is 100 more than 6235.

(b)

Thousands	Hundreds	Tens	Ones
1000 1000	100 100 100	10	1 1 1 1 1 1

100

_________ is 100 less than 2416.

2. Fill in the blanks.

(a) _________ is 10 more than 385.

(b) _________ is 10 less than 600.

(c) _________ is 100 more than 3942.

(d) _________ is 1000 less than 4507.

(e) 1083 + 100 = _________

(f) 2316 + 400 = _________

(g) 1325 − 100 = _________

(h) 4917 − 200 = _________

3. Fill in the blanks.

(a) 5409 + __________ = 5419

(b) 5409 + __________ = 6409

(c) 5409 + __________ = 5410

(d) 5409 + __________ = 5509

(e) 6998 + __________ = 7008

(f) 6998 + __________ = 7098

(g) 6998 + __________ = 7998

(h) 6998 + __________ = 6999

4. Fill in the blanks.

(a) 4864 – __________ = 4863

(b) 4864 – __________ = 4764

(c) 4864 – __________ = 3864

(d) 4864 – __________ = 4854

(e) 4050 – __________ = 4049

(f) 4050 – __________ = 3050

(g) 4050 – __________ = 3950

(h) 4050 – __________ = 4040

5. Complete the following number patterns.

(a) 3789, 3799, __________, 3819

(b) 4738, 4838, 4938, __________

(c) 987, 1987, __________, 3987

(d) __________, 1300, 1301, 1302

6. Complete the following number patterns.

(a) ________, 1301, 1300, 1299

(b) 3903, 2903, 1903, ________

(c) 4737, 4637, ________, 4437

(d) 3708, ________, 3688, 3678

7. Write the missing numbers.

4024	4034			4064
	3934			
	3834		5636	
		4634	5634	
2631		4631		
2630			5630	
	2728			3028

EXERCISE 5

1. Fill in the blanks

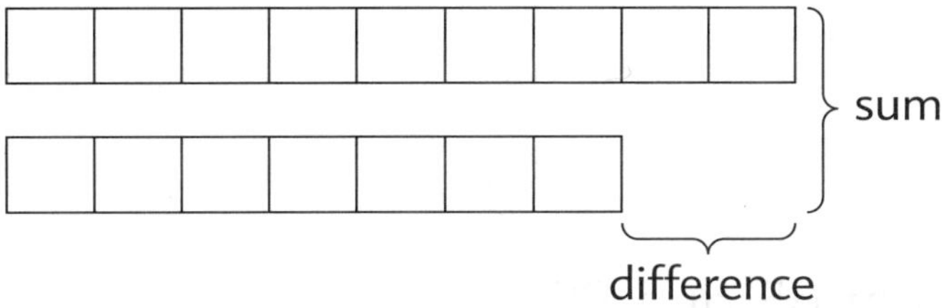

(a) $9 + 7 =$

The sum of 9 and 7 is ________.

(b) $9 - 7 =$

The difference between 9 and 7 is ________.

2.

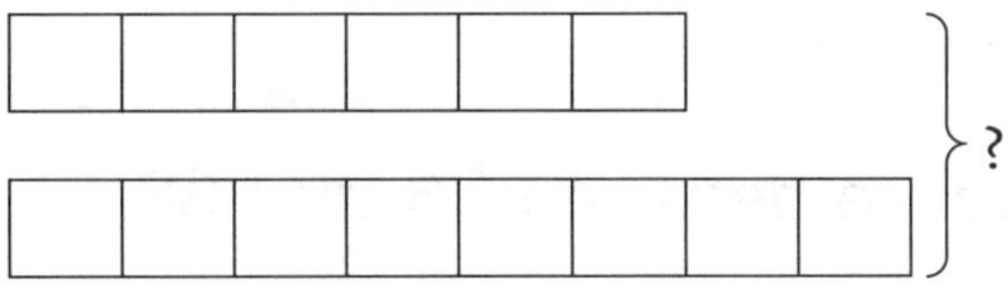

6 ○ 8 =

The sum of 6 and 8 is ________.

3.

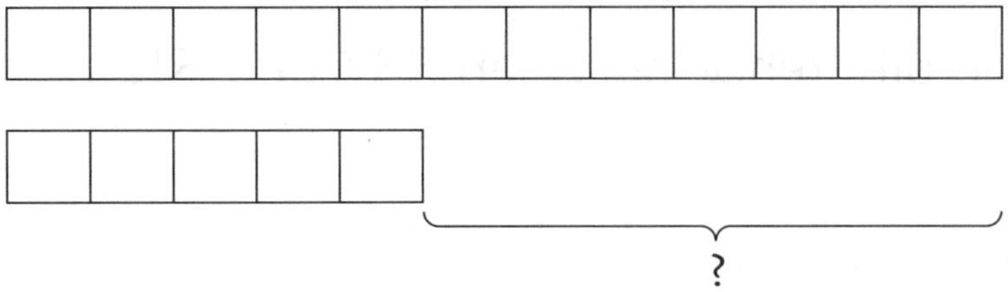

12 ○ 5 =

The difference between 12 and 5 is ________.

4. Find the sum of 65 and 89.

$65 + 89 =$

The sum of 65 and 89 is ________.

5. Find the sum of 145 and 285.

6. Find the difference between 96 and 68.

7. Find the difference between 387 and 512.

EXERCISE 6

1. Cik Halimah made 150 pineapple tarts for a party.
   After the party, there were 16 tarts left.
   How many tarts were eaten at the party?

   150 − 16 =

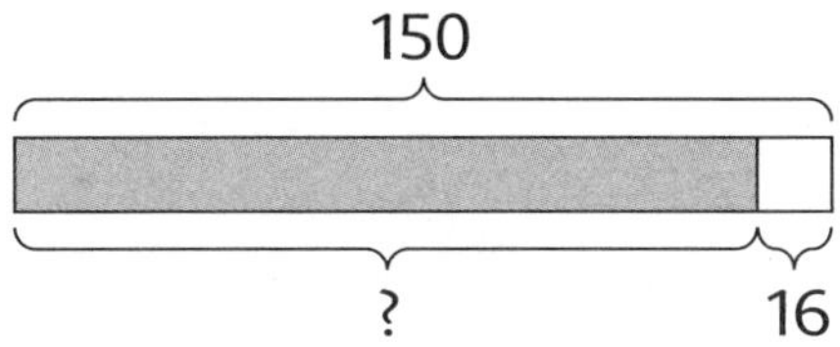

   _________ tarts were eaten at the party.

---

2. Raju's sister is 15 years old.
   How old is Raju if he is 4 years older than his sister?

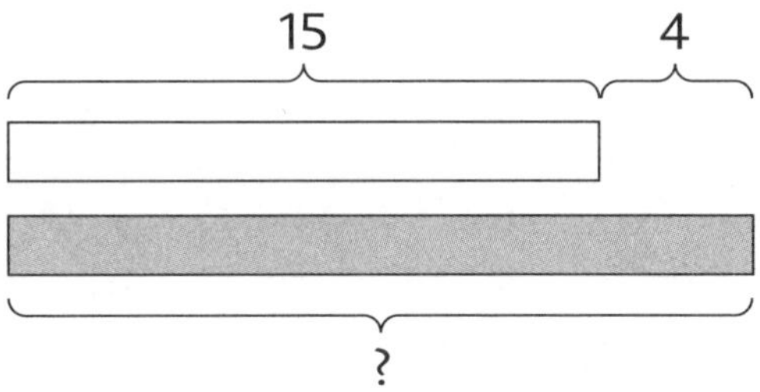

---

3. Aihua wants to wrap 42 presents for a party.
   She has wrapped 29 presents.
   How many more presents does she need to wrap?

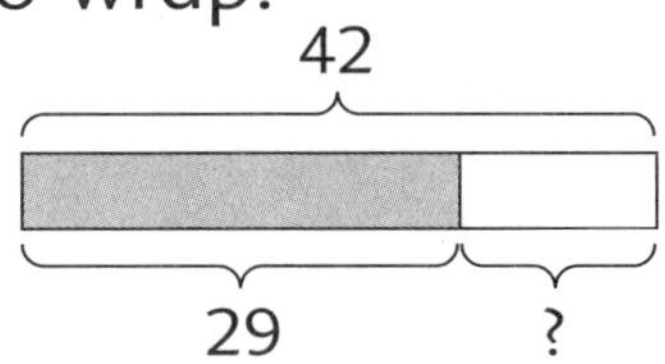

4. Rani is 12 years old.
Her sister is 21 years old.
Find the difference in age between them.

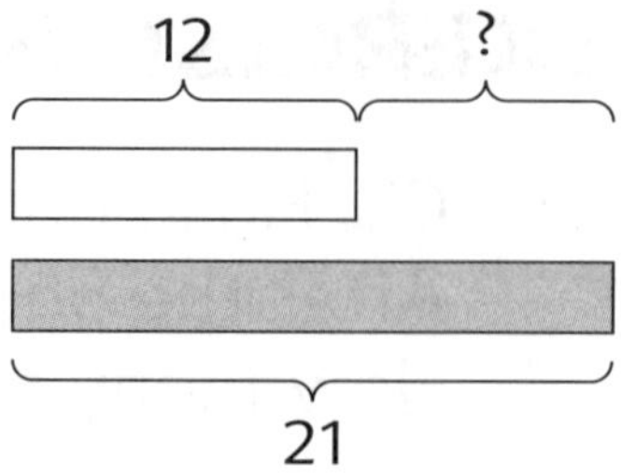

---

5. Mary weighed 39 kg last year.
She now weighs 42 kg.
How many kilograms has she gained?

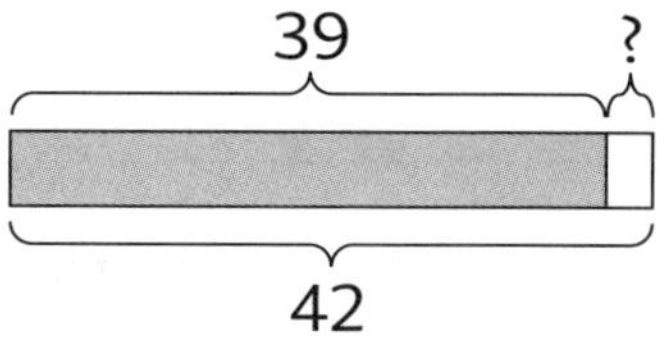

---

6. After giving away 10 comic books,
Tom had 36 comic books left.
How many comic books did Tom
have at first?

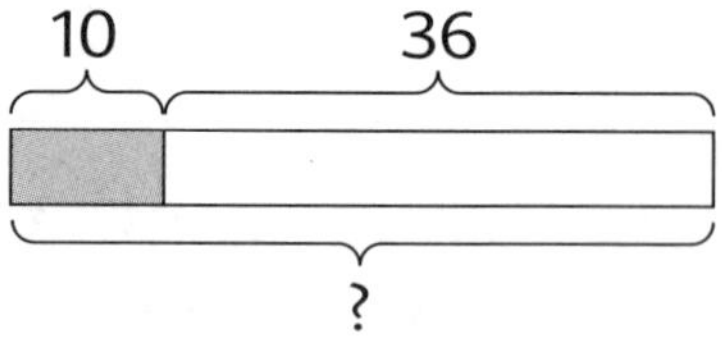

7. Mrs Wong bought a typewriter and a radio.
   She spent \$200 altogether.
   If the radio cost \$65, how much did she pay for the typewriter?

---

8. Samy is 145 cm tall.
   He is 28 cm shorter than Gopal.
   What is Gopal's height?

---

9. After giving 45 stamps to his friends, Sumin had 379 stamps left.
   How many stamps did Sumin have at first?

EXERCISE 7

1. There were 120 boys at a concert.
There were 15 more girls than boys.

(a) Write the missing numbers in the boxes.

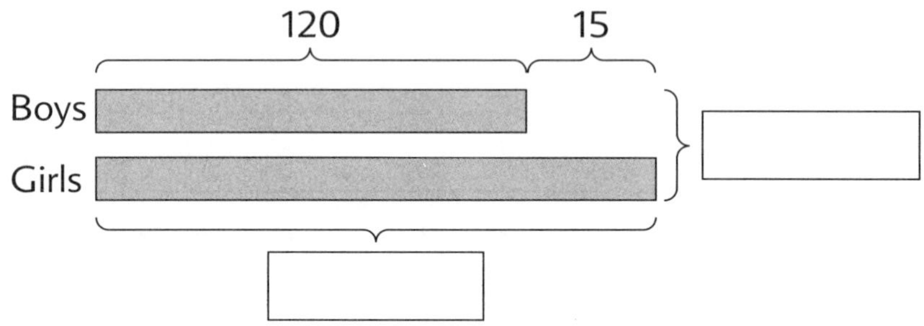

(b) How many girls were there?

(c) How many children were there altogether?

2. There are 260 members in a chess club.
136 of them are boys.

(a) Write the missing numbers in the boxes.

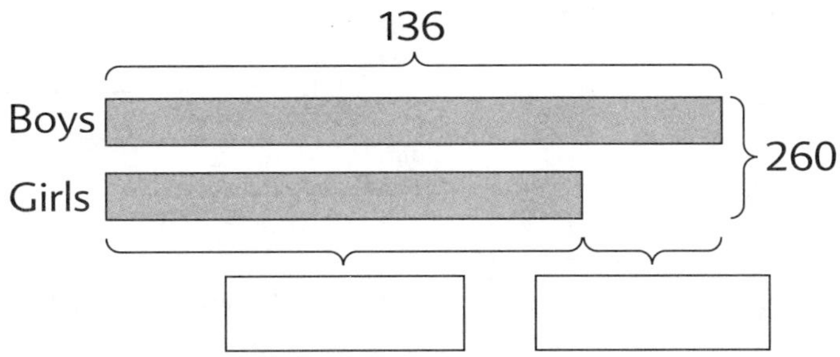

(b) How many girls are there?

(c) How many more boys than girls are there?

3. There are 72 male workers in a factory.
There are 14 fewer female workers than male workers.

(a) How many female workers are there?
(b) How many workers are there altogether?

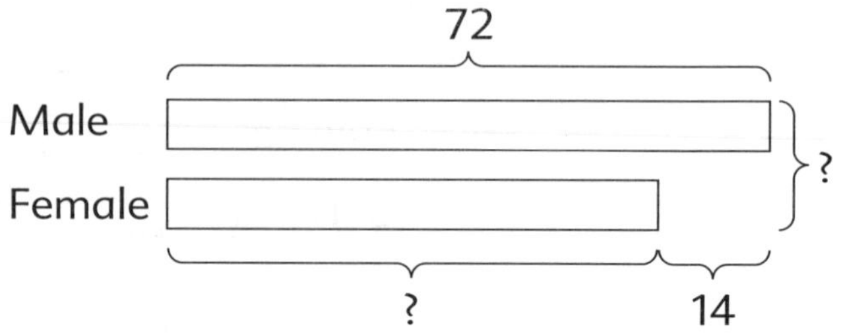

4. Mr Wu paid \$920 for a motorcycle and \$245 for a bicycle.
(a) How much did he spend altogether?
(b) How much cheaper was the bicycle than the motorcycle?

EXERCISE 8

1. Add.

3624 + 3 =

3624 + 50 =

3624 + 200 =

3624 + 4000 =

5107 + 2 =

5107 + 70 =

5107 + 600 =

5107 + 3000 =

2480 + 300 =

5243 + 50 =

4825 + 140 =

2370 + 2500 =

1934 + 4020 =

6216 + 602 =

5201 + 390 =

3402 + 4006 =

9150 + 320 =

3614 + 5320 =

2. Add.

4107 + 5 [B]	7254 + 92 [T]	1082 + 736 [E]
1902 + 4563 [S]	3058 + 16 [V]	7620 + 671 [L]
5108 + 4829 [E]	3443 + 2270 [A]	6355 + 824 [G]

What tables do we eat?

Write the letters which match the answers above to find out.

						B			
3074	1818	7179	1818	7346	5713	4112	8291	9937	6465

3. There are 2618 adults and 1254 children at a concert.
   How many people are there altogether?

   2618 + 1254 =

   There are ________ people altogether.

---

4. David collected 3546 stamps.
   Weihua collected 632 more stamps than David.
   How many stamps did Weihua collect?

---

5. After delivering 1430 letters, a postman still had 390 letters to deliver.
   How many letters were there altogether?

EXERCISE 9

1. Add.

A. $\begin{array}{r} 2067 \\ +\ 4594 \\ \hline \end{array}$	B. $\begin{array}{r} 2387 \\ +\ 6805 \\ \hline \end{array}$	C. $\begin{array}{r} 3247 \\ +\ 1968 \\ \hline \end{array}$
D. $\begin{array}{r} 2594 \\ +\ \ \ 533 \\ \hline \end{array}$	E. $\begin{array}{r} 4396 \\ +\ 2895 \\ \hline \end{array}$	F. $\begin{array}{r} 9076 \\ +\ \ \ 348 \\ \hline \end{array}$
G. $\begin{array}{r} 4828 \\ +\ 3864 \\ \hline \end{array}$	H. $\begin{array}{r} 3769 \\ +\ \ \ 385 \\ \hline \end{array}$	I. $\begin{array}{r} 1346 \\ +\ 5914 \\ \hline \end{array}$

Join the dots by following the order of the answers above.

You will get a picture of a ________.

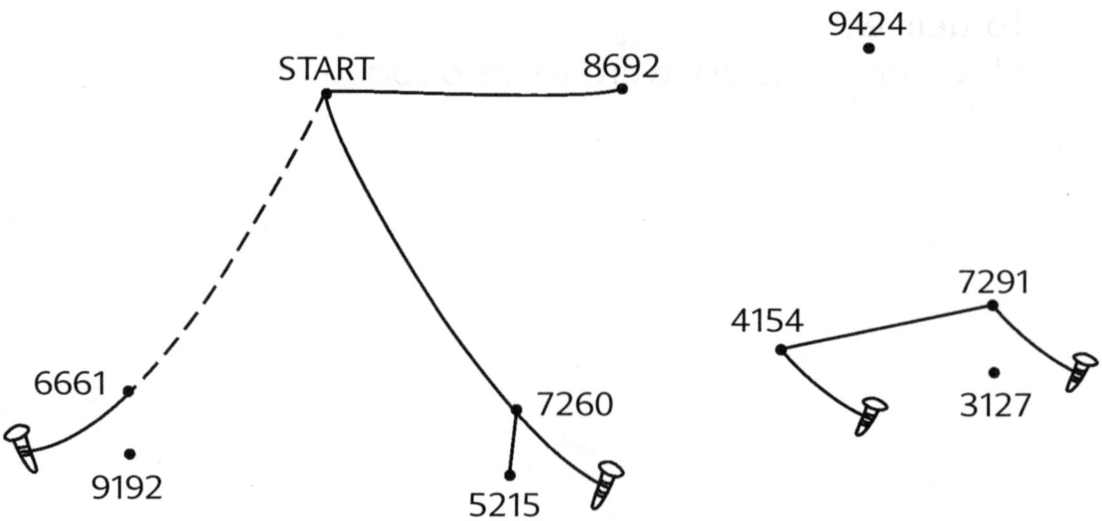

2. 2176 people attended a concert on the first night.
2745 people attended the concert on the second night.
How many people attended the concert on both nights?

---

3. After paying $1138 for a television set, Mr Chan had $862 left.
How much money did he have at first?

---

4. A computer costs $1685.
It is $425 cheaper than a piano.
What is the cost of the piano?

EXERCISE 10

1. Subtract

9324 − 2	6547 − 29	7647 − 247
1589 − 1314	4146 − 833	9045 − 811
5691 − 455	4393 − 1800	2752 − 1492

Colour only the boxes which contain the answers.
What letter does it show?

2901	2593	4993	6518	9326
313	7400	8324	3313	5833
9084	5236	8526	1260	6558
7800	275	9322	8234	4579

2. There were 2546 adults and 1037 children at a concert.
How many more adults than children were there?

---

3. Ailian had $1860.
She spent $1248 and saved the rest.
How much did she save?

---

4. Meihua collected 3586 saga seeds.
She collected 1864 more saga seeds than Sufen.
How many saga seeds did Sufen collect?

EXERCISE 11

1. Subtract

①	②	③
9474 − 86	9835 − 246	4066 − 1737

④	⑤	⑥
2435 − 919	3962 − 465	2412 − 1283

⑦	⑧	⑨
9731 − 1537	8340 − 82	6538 − 2809

Be ******* at all times.**

Write the letters which match the answers.
You will find the missing word.

C — 9388	E — 1129	R — 1516
U — 2329	S — 3729	O — 9589
T — 3497	O — 8194	U — 8258

C								
①	②	③	④	⑤	⑥	⑦	⑧	⑨

2. Subtract

9238 − 966 ①	3533 − 584 ②	6147 − 4275 ③
8260 − 2475 ④	7371 − 585 ⑤	4216 − 1379 ⑥
7152 − 2426 ⑦	9542 − 5683 ⑧	7930 − 247 ⑨

Write the letters which match the answers.
You will find the name of a fruit.

A — 2949
R — 2837
F — 6786

K — 5785
T — 7683
C — 1872

U — 4726
I — 3859
J — 8272

J								
①	②	③	④	⑤	⑥	⑦	⑧	⑨

EXERCISE 12

1. Subtract and write the answers in the boxes.

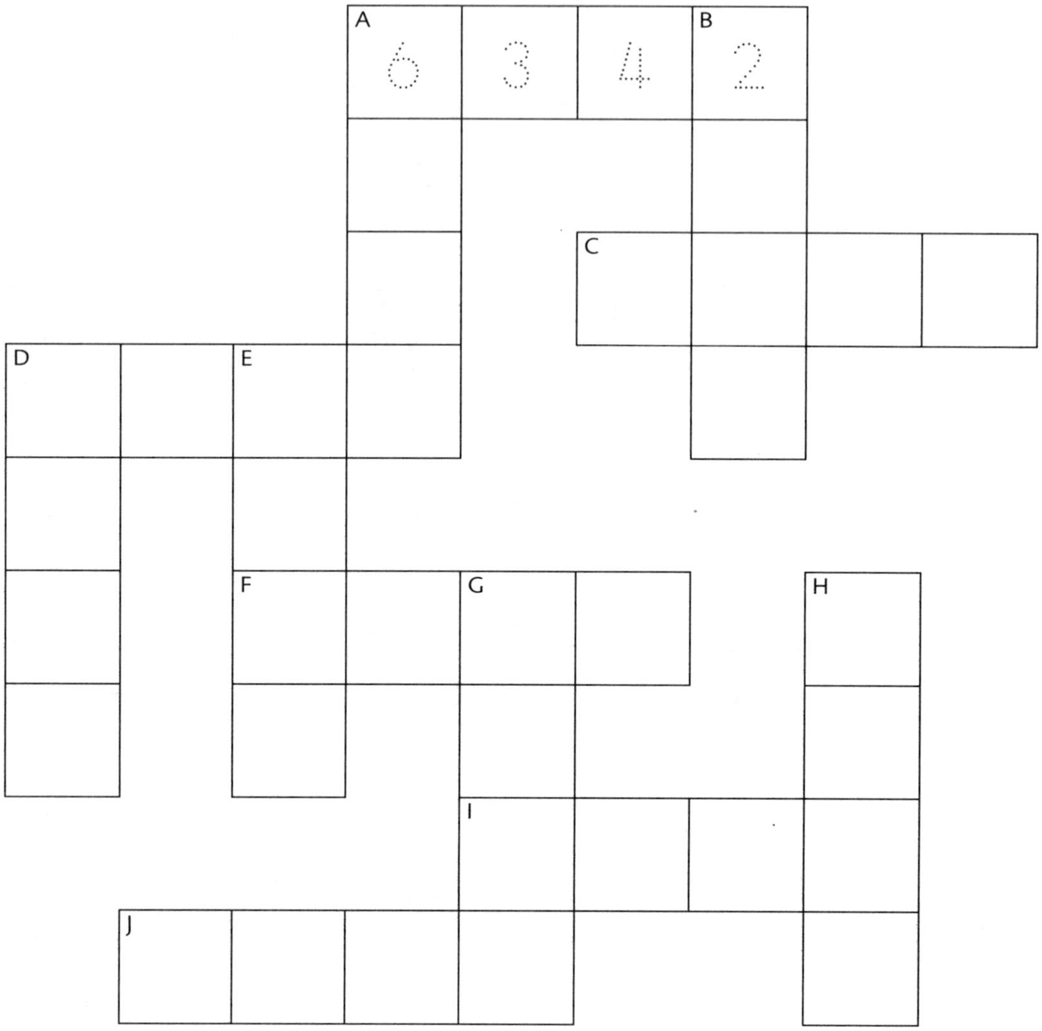

Across

A. 9101 – 2759

C. 8290 – 4986

D. 6000 – 486

F. 9400 – 6869

I. 5102 – 897

J. 6400 – 4439

Down

A. 7032 – 778

B. 8070 – 5635

D. 7968 – 2240

E. 4005 – 2678

G. 7533 – 4492

H. 8144 – 485

2. A school library had 2040 books.
   1458 of them had been borrowed.
   How many books were left in the library?

---

3. A bookshop has 3690 cards for sale.
   1861 of them are birthday cards.
   How many are **not** birthday cards?

---

4. A worker needs 3606 bricks to build a house.
   He has 2679 bricks now.
   How many more bricks must he get?

EXERCISE 13

1. David ordered 1500 sticks of chicken satay and 850 sticks of beef satay for a party.
   264 sticks of satay were left after the party.
   How many sticks of satay were eaten at the party?

---

2. Mr Lin sold 654 durians on Saturday.
   He sold 346 more durians on Sunday than on Saturday.
   How many durians were sold on both days?

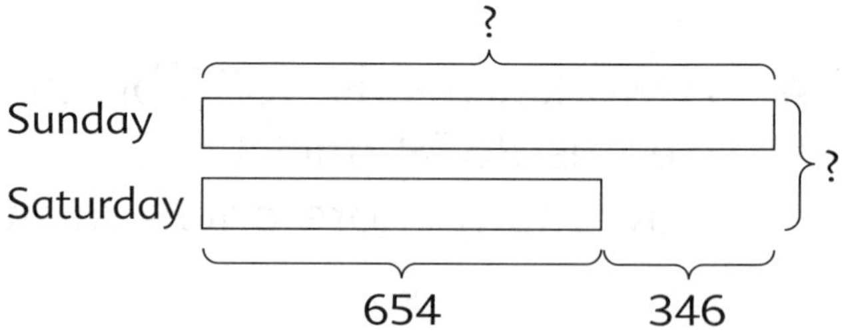

3. There were 3245 people at a parade.
1400 of them were men, 980 were women.
How many children were there?

---

4. Devi saved $1435.
Meilin saved $298 more than Devi.
Alice saved $325 less than Meilin.
How much did Alice save?

5. A factory has 2000 workers.
   1340 of them are men.
   The rest are women.
   How many more men than women are there?

---

6. The total cost of an oven and a refrigerator is \$2030.
   The oven costs \$695.
   Find the difference between the costs of the oven and refrigerator.

REVISION 1

1. Fill in the blanks.
   (a) 200 + 70 + 1 = ________
   (b) 5000 + 700 + 2 = ________
   (c) 892 = ________ + 90 + 2
   (d) 3073 = 3000 + ________ + 3

2. Fill in the blanks with the words **greater** or **smaller**.
   (a) 756 is ________ than 675.
   (b) 860 is ________ than 856.
   (c) 7000 is ________ than 6999.
   (d) 1055 is ________ than 1155.
   (e) 9005 is ________ than 9050.
   (f) 10 000 is ________ than 9999.

3. (a) In 90**2**7, the value of the digit **2** is ________.
   (b) In 2458, the digit ________ is in the **hundreds place**.
   (c) In 3246, the digit in the **thousands place** is ________.

4. Fill in the blanks.
   (a) 350 is 10 more than ________.
   (b) 218 is 100 less than ________.
   (c) 6875 is 1000 more than ________.
   (d) ________ is 10 less than 525.
   (e) ________ is 100 less than 970.
   (f) ________ is 1000 more than 7061.

5. The numbers on each side of the triangle add up to 1000.
Write the missing numbers.

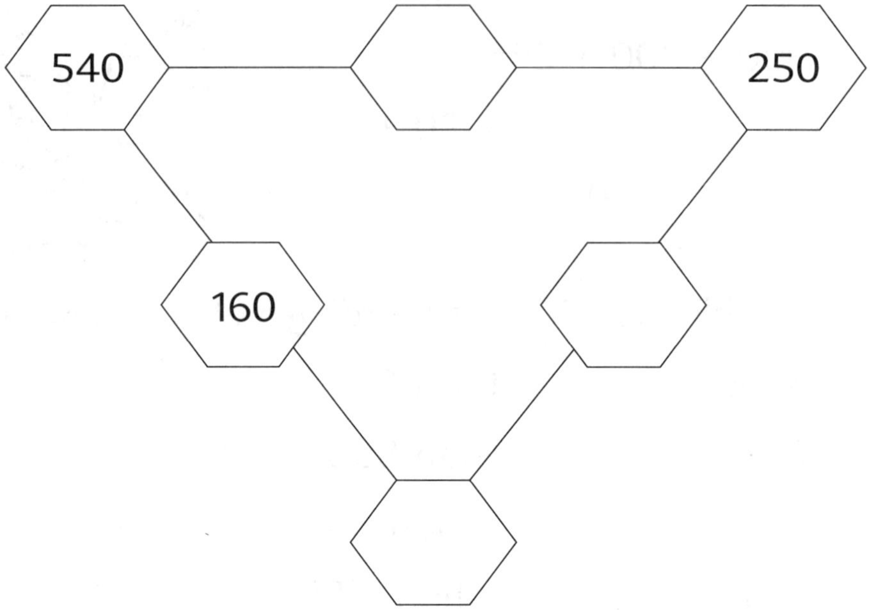

6. Write the missing numbers.

(a) 2034 $\xrightarrow{+1000}$ ☐ $\xrightarrow{+200}$ ☐

2034 + 1200 =

(b) 3888 $\xrightarrow{-2000}$ ☐ $\xrightarrow{-80}$ ☐

3888 − 2080 =

(c) 4852 $\xrightarrow{+600}$ ☐ $\xrightarrow{+8}$ ☐

4852 + 608 =

(d) 3604 $\xrightarrow{-800}$ ☐ $\xrightarrow{-50}$ ☐

3604 − 850 =

7. After reading 1445 pages of a book, Mrs Chen still has 258 pages to read.
How many pages are there in the book?

8. There were 3521 people at a funfair.
2868 of them were adults.
How many children were there?

9. Mr Fu wants to buy a motorcycle which costs $5430.
He has $3350.
How much more money does he need?

10. Mrs Wu had $2790.
She spent $1430 on a refrigerator and $890 on a television set.
How much money had she left?

---

11. A postman delivered 1050 letters on Monday.
He delivered 206 fewer letters on Tuesday than on Monday.
How many letters did he deliver on both days?

EXERCISE 14

1. Write the numbers.

(a)

4 sixes =

(b)

3 fives =

(c)

2 groups of 4 =

(d)

5 groups of 3 =

2. Complete the tables.

(a) There are 3 feathers on a hat.

Number of hats	1	2	3	4	5
Number of feathers	3	6			

(b) A rabbit has 4 legs.

Number of rabbits	1	2	3	4	5
Number of legs	4	8			

(c) A flower has 5 petals.

Number of flowers	1	2	3	4	5
Number of petals	5	10			

3. Complete the number patterns.

(a) 2, 4, 6, ______, ______, ______, 14, ______, 18, 20.

(b) 3, 6, 9, ______, ______, ______, 21, ______, 27, 30.

(c) 4, 8, 12, ______, ______, 24, ______, ______, ______, 40.

(d) 5, 10, 15, ______, ______, 30, ______, ______, 45, 50.

(e) 10, 20, 30, ______, ______, 60, ______, ______, 90, 100.

EXERCISE 15

1. There are 9 bees in each group.

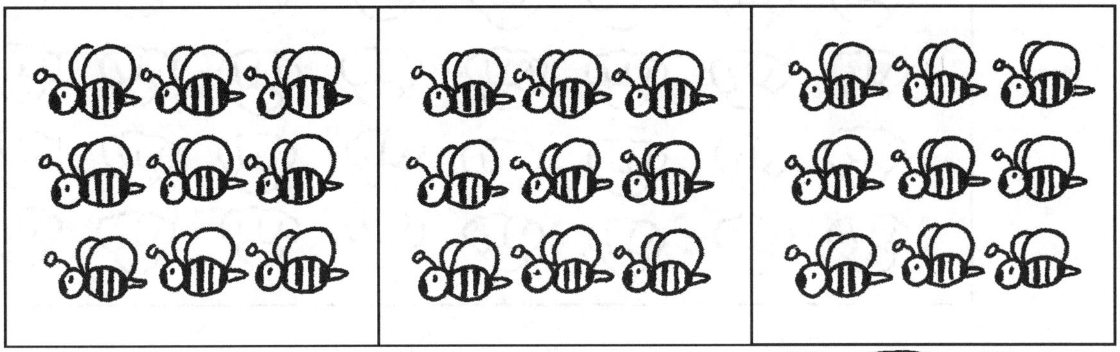

$9 \times 3 =$

There are ________ bees altogether.

2. Complete the following sentences.

(a)

5 multiplied by 3 = ☐ 3 groups of 5 = ☐

(b)

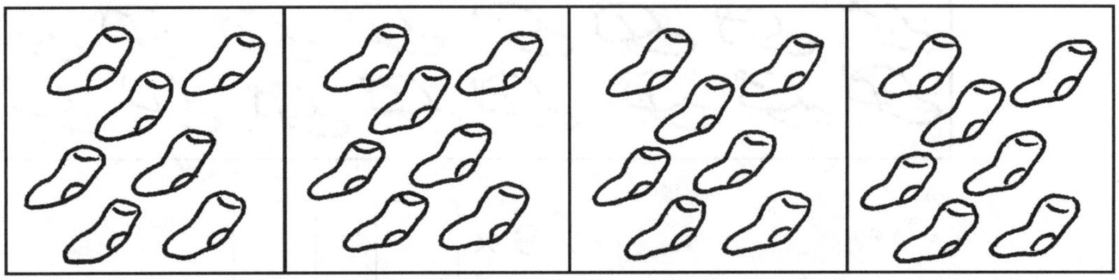

$7 \times 4 =$ ☐ $7 + 7 + 7 + 7 =$ ☐

3. Complete the following sentences.

(a)

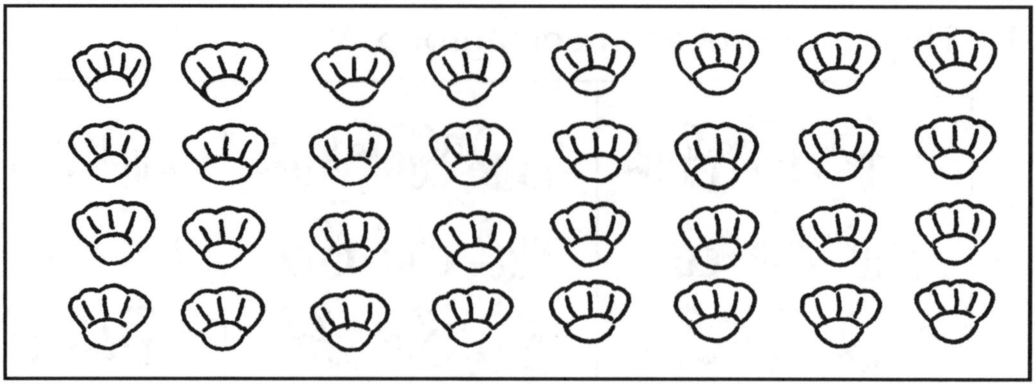

$8 \times 4 = \square$

$4 \times 8 = \square$

(b)

$6 \times 2 = \square$

$2 \times 6 = \square$

(c)

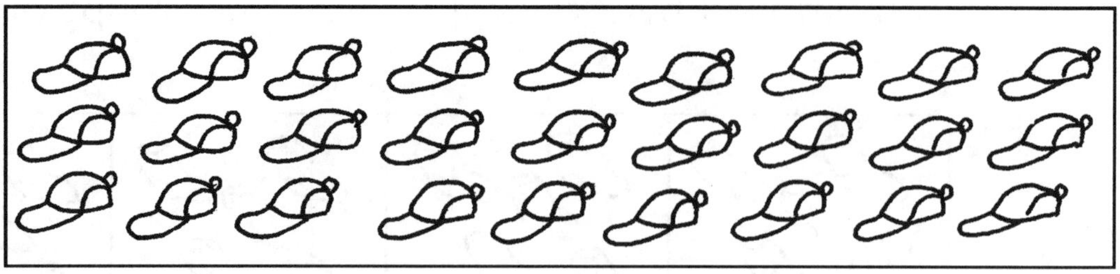

$9 \times \square = \square$

$3 \times \square = \square$

EXERCISE 16

1. There are 12 birds altogether.

(a) 

Divide 12 birds into 3 equal groups.
How many birds are there in each group?

$12 \div 3 =$

There are ________ birds in each group.

(b) Divide 12 birds into groups of 4.
How many groups are there?

$12 \div 4 =$

There are ________ groups.

2. Complete the division sentences.

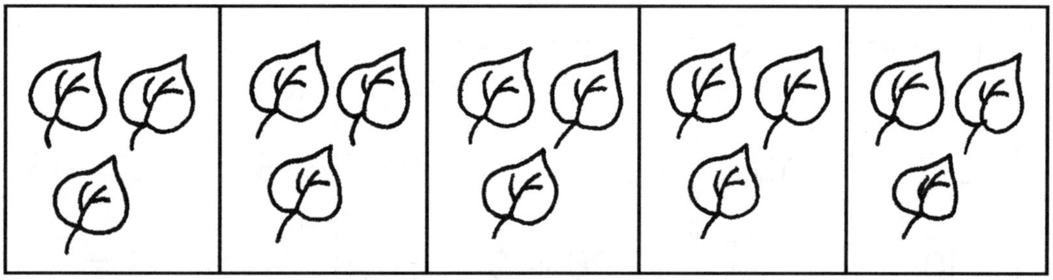

$15 \div 3 = \square$ $15 \div 5 = \square$

3. Complete the number sentences on each bottle.

$6 \times 2 = 12$

$12 \div 2 =$ ____

____ $\times 2 = 18$

$18 \div 2 =$ ____

$2 \times$ ____ $= 10$

$10 \div 2 =$ ____

____ $\times 3 = 21$

$21 \div 3 =$ ____

$3 \times$ ____ $= 27$

$27 \div 3 =$ ____

____ $\times 3 = 15$

$15 \div 3 =$ ____

$4 \times$ ____ $= 24$

$24 \div 4 =$ ____

____ $\times 4 = 36$

$36 \div 4 =$ ____

____ $\times 4 = 32$

$32 \div 4 =$ ____

____ $\times 5 = 10$

$10 \div 5 =$ ____

____ $\times 5 = 30$

$30 \div 5 =$ ____

$5 \times$ ____ $= 45$

$45 \div 5 =$ ____

4. Divide.

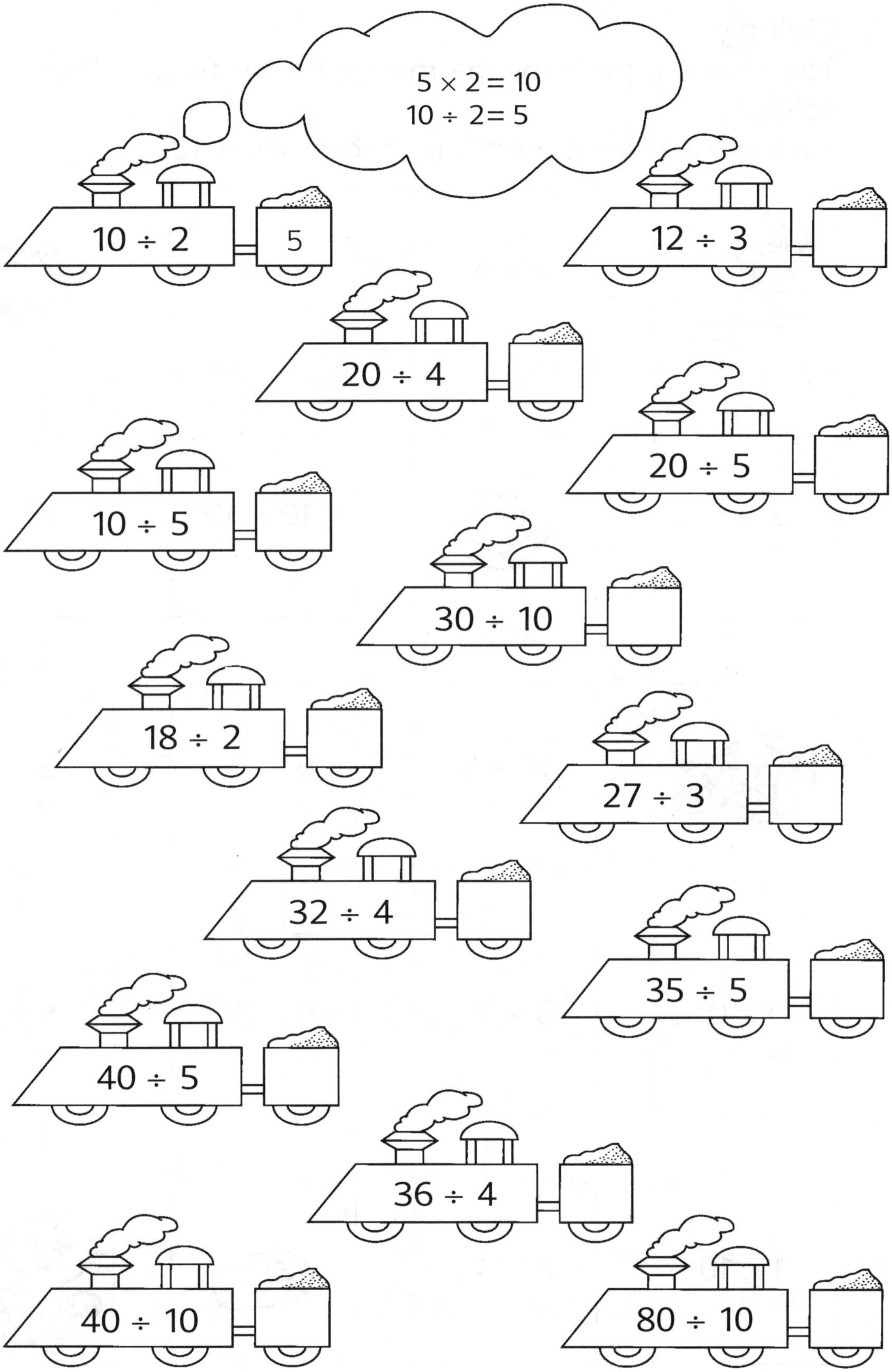
5 × 2 = 10
10 ÷ 2 = 5
10 ÷ 2
5
12 ÷ 3
20 ÷ 4
20 ÷ 5
10 ÷ 5
30 ÷ 10
18 ÷ 2
27 ÷ 3
32 ÷ 4
35 ÷ 5
40 ÷ 5
36 ÷ 4
40 ÷ 10
80 ÷ 10

EXERCISE 17

1. Multiply.
   Then trace a path for the mouse to get to the cheese safely.
   Each answer on the path is greater than 12.

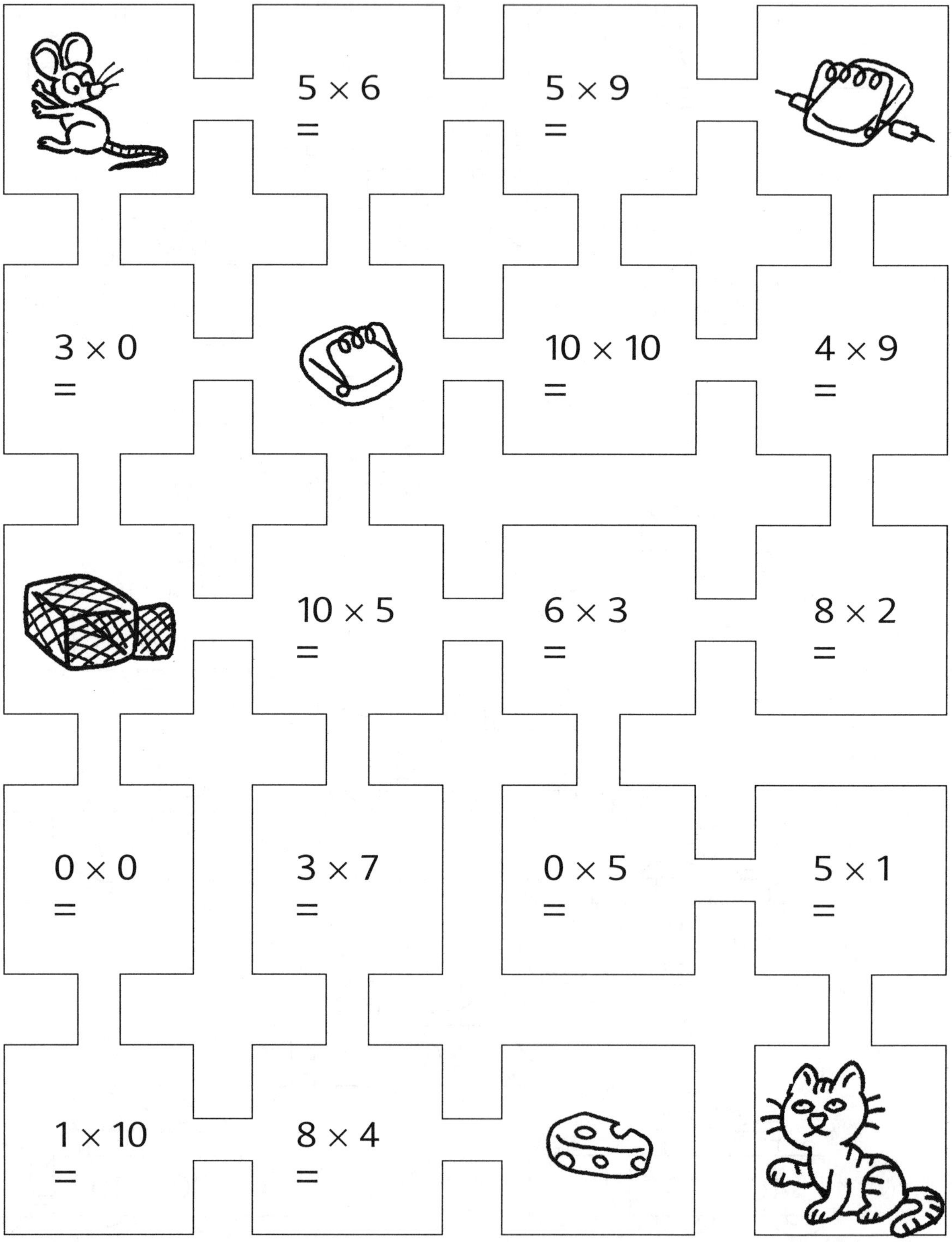

2. Divide.

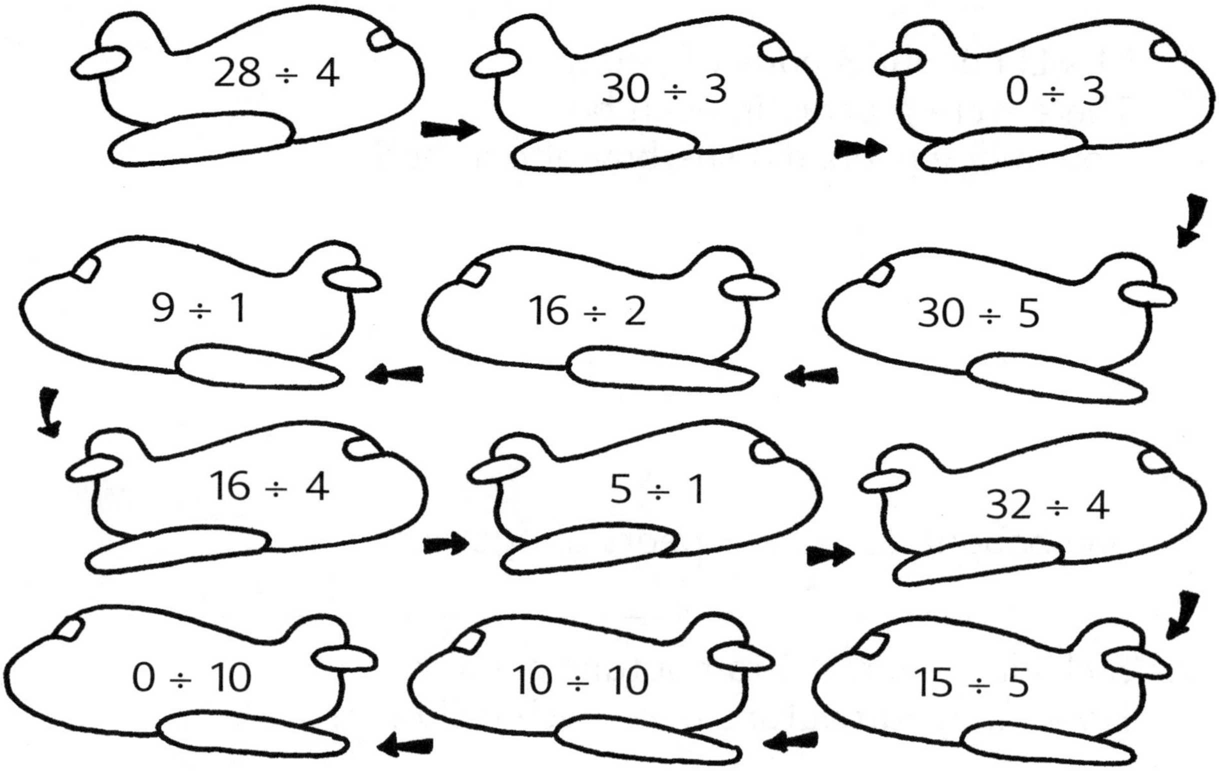

Trace a path through the maze by following the order of the answers above.

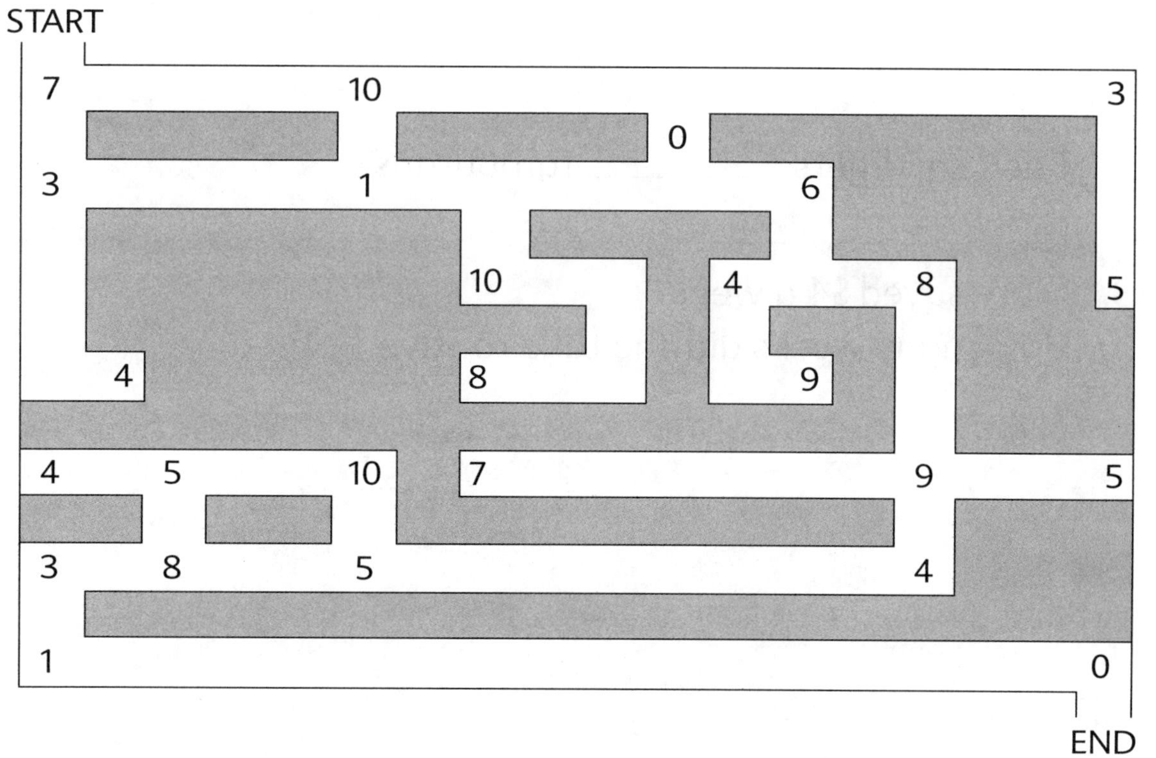

EXERCISE 18

1. Mrs Li bought 3 bags of pears.
   There were 4 pears in each bag.
   How many pears did she buy altogether?

   She bought ________ pears altogether.

---

2. 5 children share 40 rambutans equally.
   How many rambutans does each child get?

   Each child gets ________ rambutans.

---

3. Mary saved $4 a week.
   How many weeks did she take to save $24?

4. Mingli earned $45 in 5 days.
He earned the same amount each day.
How much did he earn a day?

---

5. A tailor made 8 dresses.
He used 3 m of cloth for each dress.
How much cloth did he use in all?

---

6. Mr Wu bought 6 tubs of ice cream.
Each tub contained 2 litres of ice cream.
How many litres of ice cream did he buy?

EXERCISE 19

1. Roy had 3 times as many comic books as Samy.
   If Samy had 7 comic books, how many comic books did Roy have?

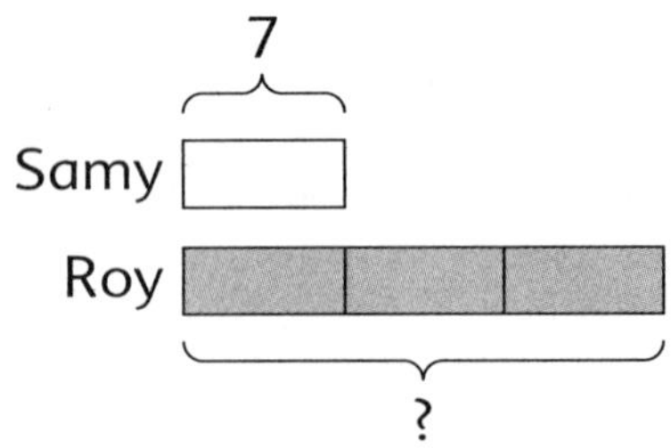

   Roy had ________ comic books.

---

2. Mingli saved \$32 in 4 weeks.
   He saved the same amount of money each week.
   How much did he save a week?

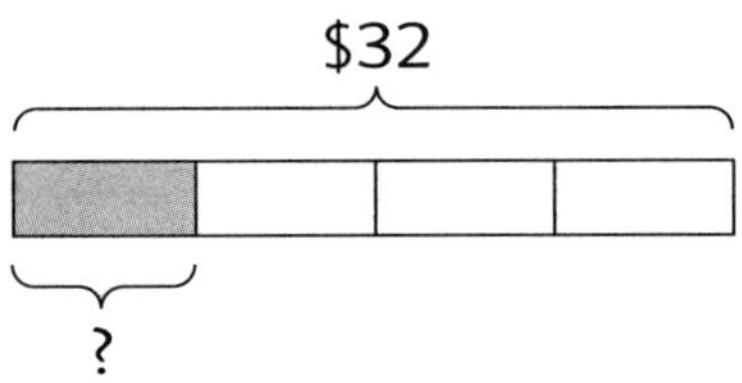

---

3. There are 20 monkeys in a zoo.
   There are 4 times as many monkeys as tigers.
   How many tigers are there?

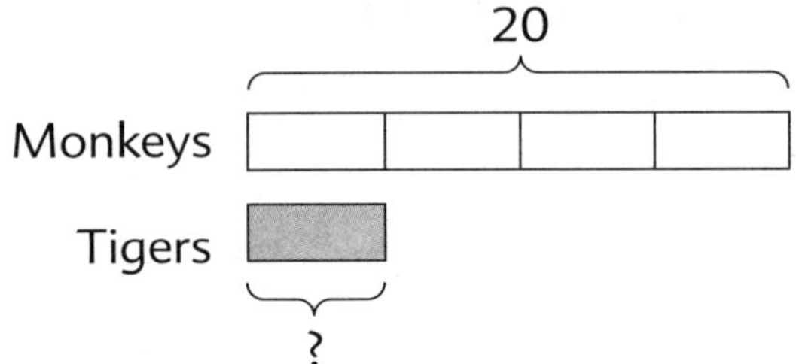

4. A toy car costs $5.
A toy aeroplane costs 4 times as much as the toy car.

(a) Write the missing numbers in the boxes.

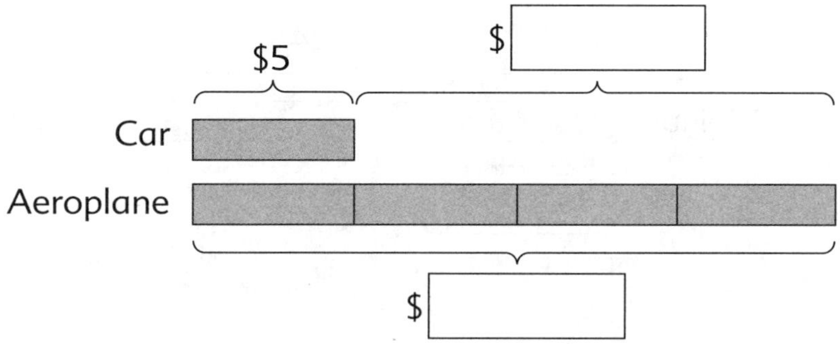

(b) What is the cost of the toy aeroplane?

(c) How much more does the toy aeroplane cost than the toy car?

5. Meihua saved $24.
She saved 3 times as much as Weilin.

(a) Write the missing numbers in the boxes.

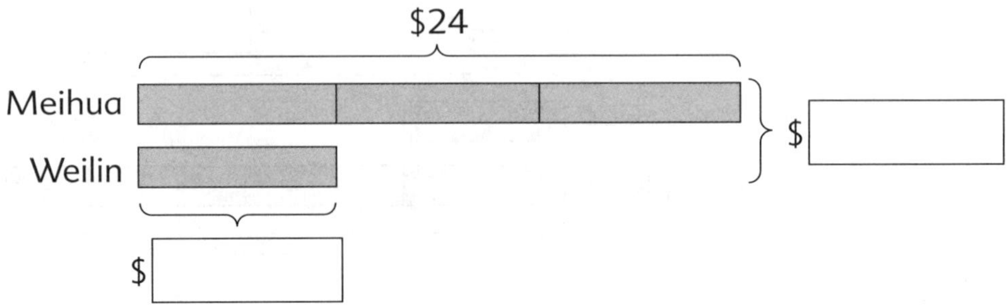

(b) How much did Weilin save?

(c) How much did Meihua and Weilin save altogether?

EXERCISE 20

1. Meiling reads 8 pages of a book a day.
   After reading the book for 4 days, she still has 5 pages to read.
   How many pages are there in the book?

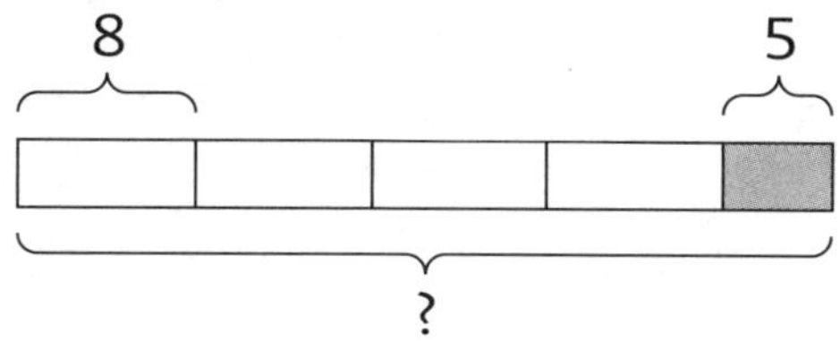

---

2. Rani had \$47.
   After paying for 3 kg of prawns, she had \$20 left.
   Find the cost of 1 kg of prawns.

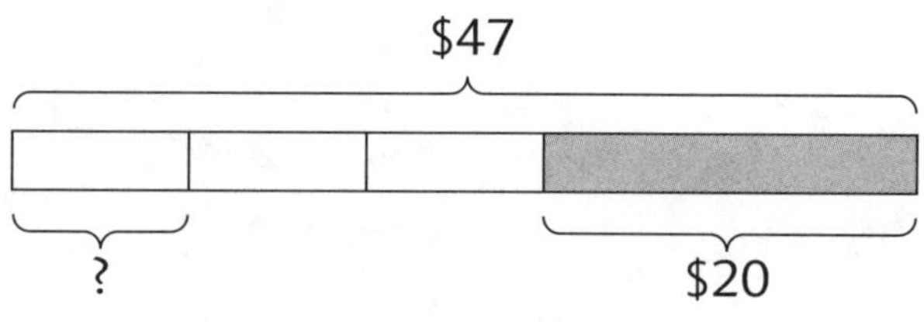

3. Mary bought 8 apples.
She bought twice as many oranges as apples.
How many more oranges than apples did she buy?

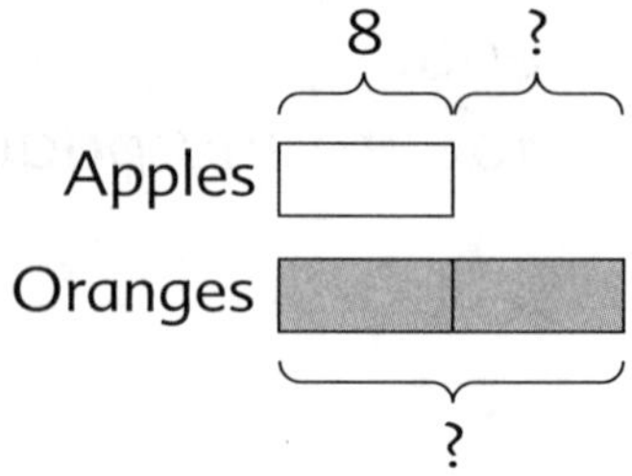

4. A pole is 3 m long.
A rope is 8 times as long as the pole.
If the rope is divided equally into 4 pieces, what is the length of each piece of rope?

EXERCISE 21

1. Multiply.

$$\begin{array}{r} 6 \\ \times\ 2 \\ \hline \end{array} \qquad \begin{array}{r} 60 \\ \times\ \ 2 \\ \hline \end{array} \qquad \begin{array}{r} 7 \\ \times\ 3 \\ \hline \end{array} \qquad \begin{array}{r} 70 \\ \times\ \ 3 \\ \hline \end{array}$$

$$\begin{array}{r} 3 \\ \times\ 5 \\ \hline \end{array} \qquad \begin{array}{r} 30 \\ \times\ \ 5 \\ \hline \end{array} \qquad \begin{array}{r} 5 \\ \times\ 4 \\ \hline \end{array} \qquad \begin{array}{r} 50 \\ \times\ \ 4 \\ \hline \end{array}$$

$$\begin{array}{r} 9 \\ \times\ 2 \\ \hline \end{array} \qquad \begin{array}{r} 900 \\ \times\ \ \ 2 \\ \hline \end{array} \qquad \begin{array}{r} 8 \\ \times\ 3 \\ \hline \end{array} \qquad \begin{array}{r} 800 \\ \times\ \ \ 3 \\ \hline \end{array}$$

$$\begin{array}{r} 7 \\ \times\ 4 \\ \hline \end{array} \qquad \begin{array}{r} 700 \\ \times\ \ \ 4 \\ \hline \end{array} \qquad \begin{array}{r} 6 \\ \times\ 4 \\ \hline \end{array} \qquad \begin{array}{r} 600 \\ \times\ \ \ 5 \\ \hline \end{array}$$

2. Multiply.

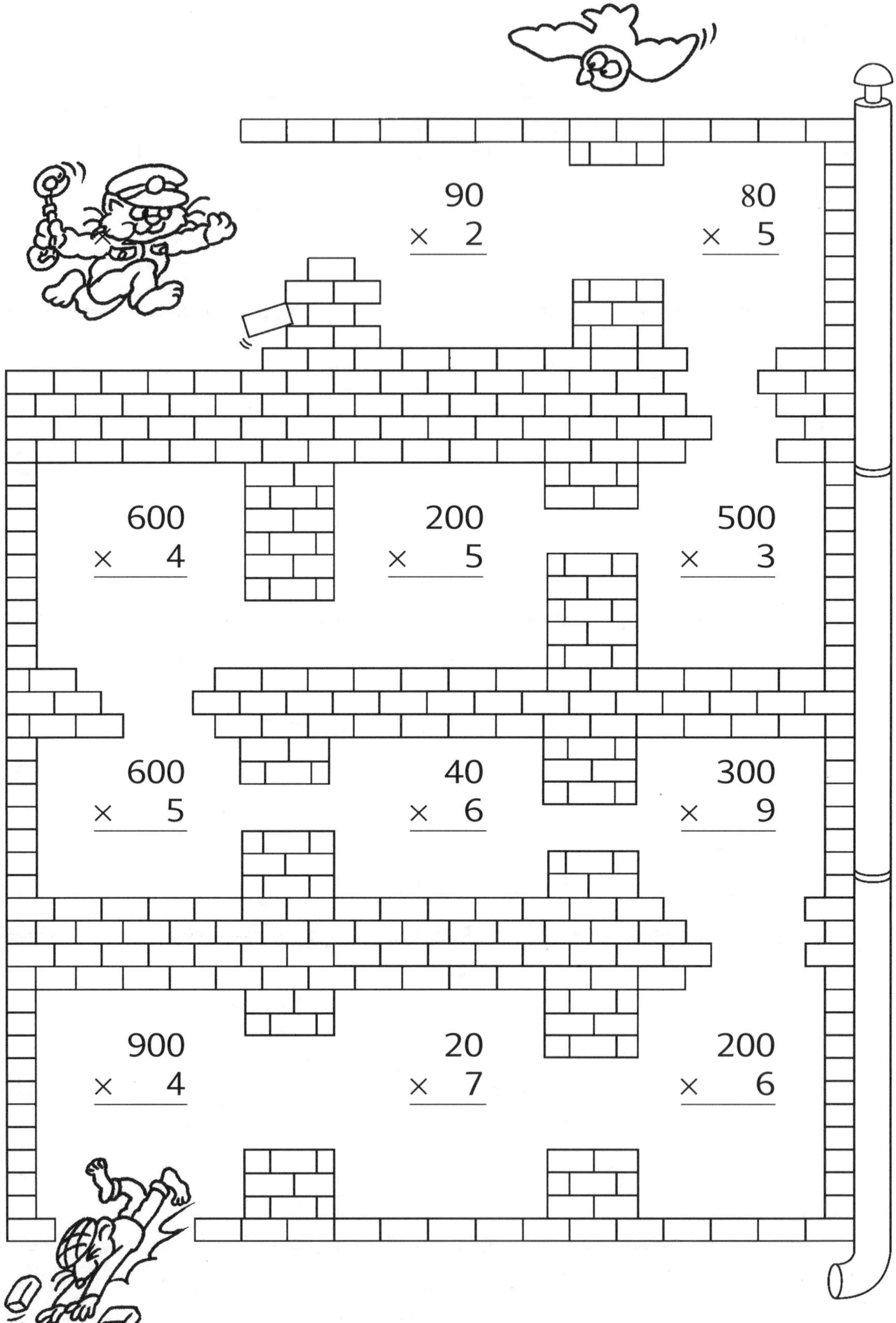

	90×2	80×5
600×4	200×5	500×3
600×5	40×6	300×9
900×4	20×7	200×6

EXERCISE 22

1. Multiply.

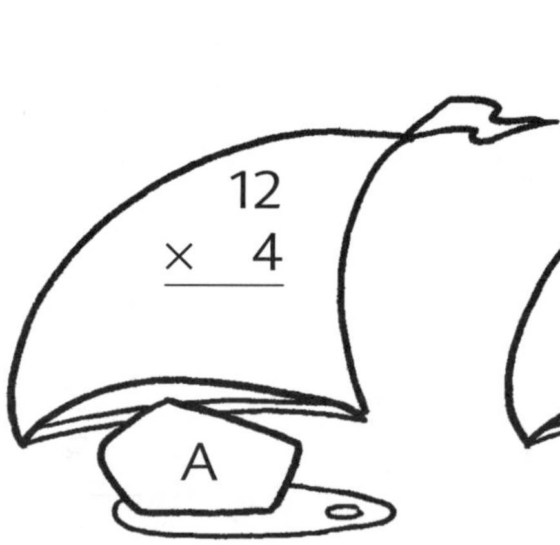

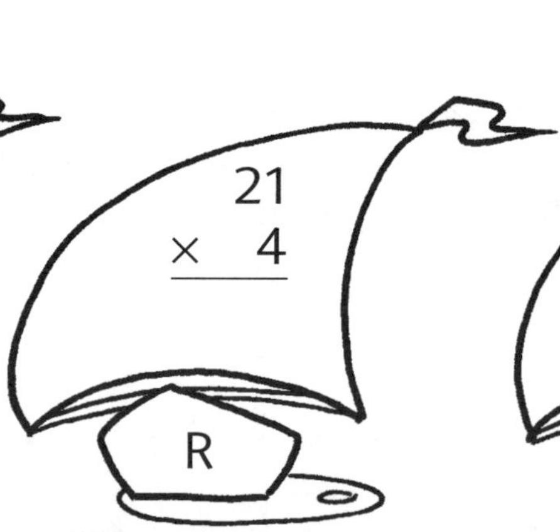

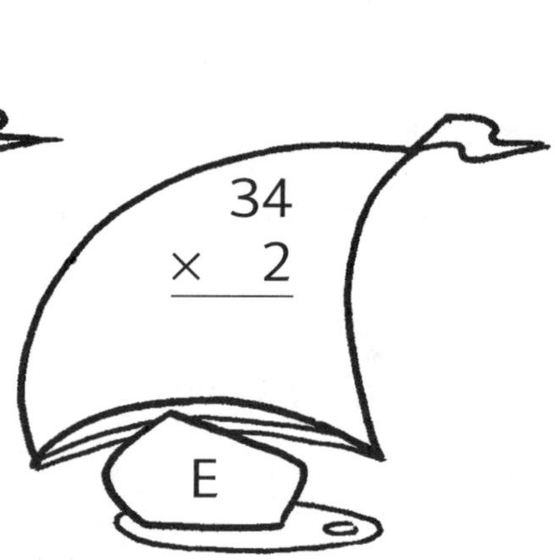

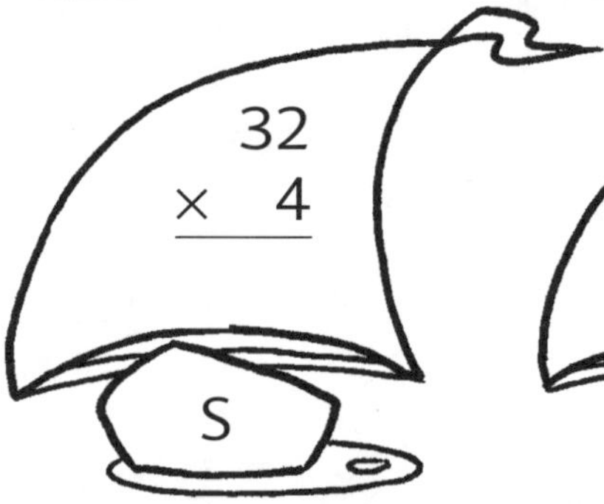

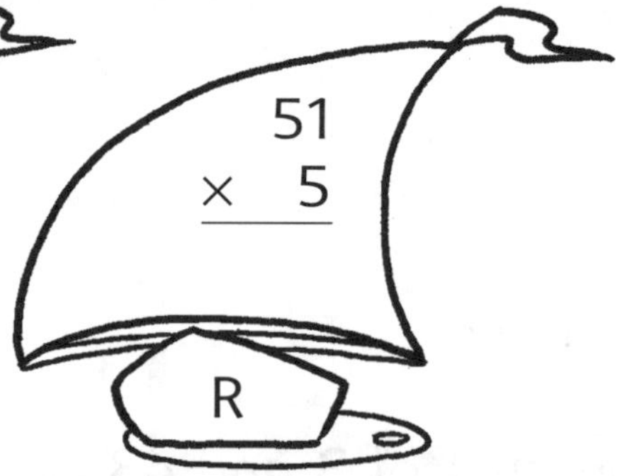

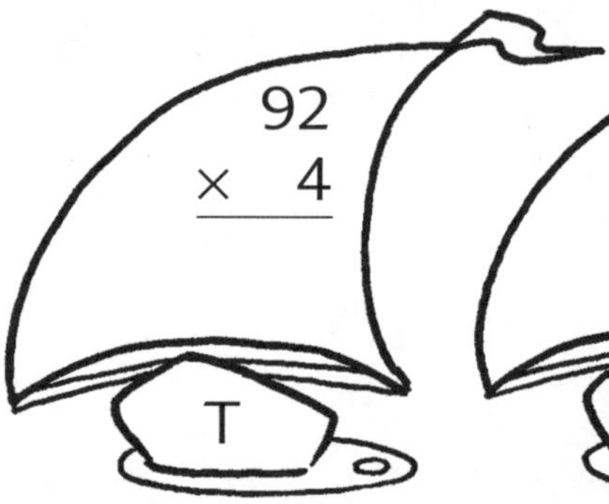

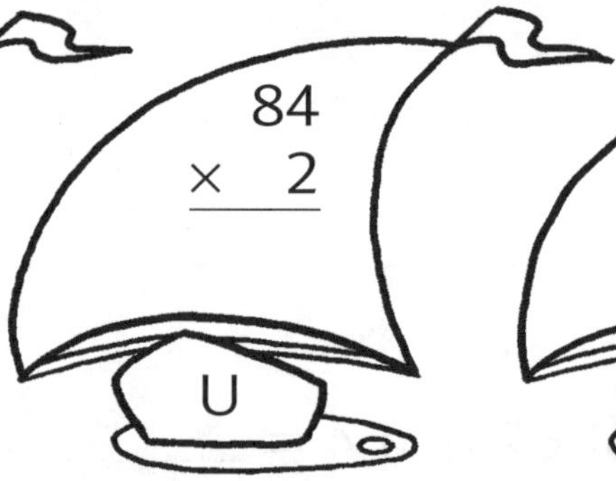

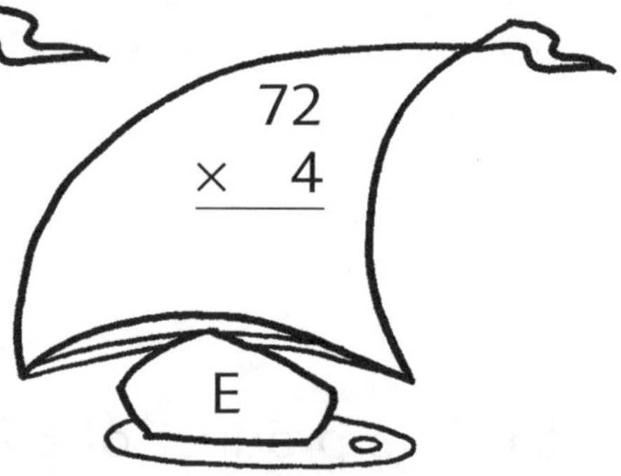

Where are the boats sailing to?

Write the letters which match the answers to find out.

			A				
368	84	68	48	128	168	255	288

ISLAND

2. Find the product for each of the following.

(a) $41 \times 5 =$ ________

$$\begin{array}{r} 41 \\ \times \quad 5 \\ \hline \\ \hline \end{array}$$

(b) $3 \times 52 =$ ________

$$\begin{array}{r} 52 \\ \times \quad 3 \\ \hline \\ \hline \end{array}$$

3. Fill in the blanks.

(a) The product of 3 and 43 = ________

$$\begin{array}{r} 43 \\ \times \quad 3 \\ \hline \\ \hline \end{array}$$

(b) The product of 62 and 4 = ________

(c) The product of 5 and 71 = ________

EXERCISE 23

1. Multiply.

37 × 2	45 × 3	58 × 2	86 × 4
37 × 5	23 × 5	32 × 3	57 × 4
65 × 3	43 × 2	79 × 4	98 × 5

Colour the spaces which contain the answers above.
They will lead you to where the treasure is buried.

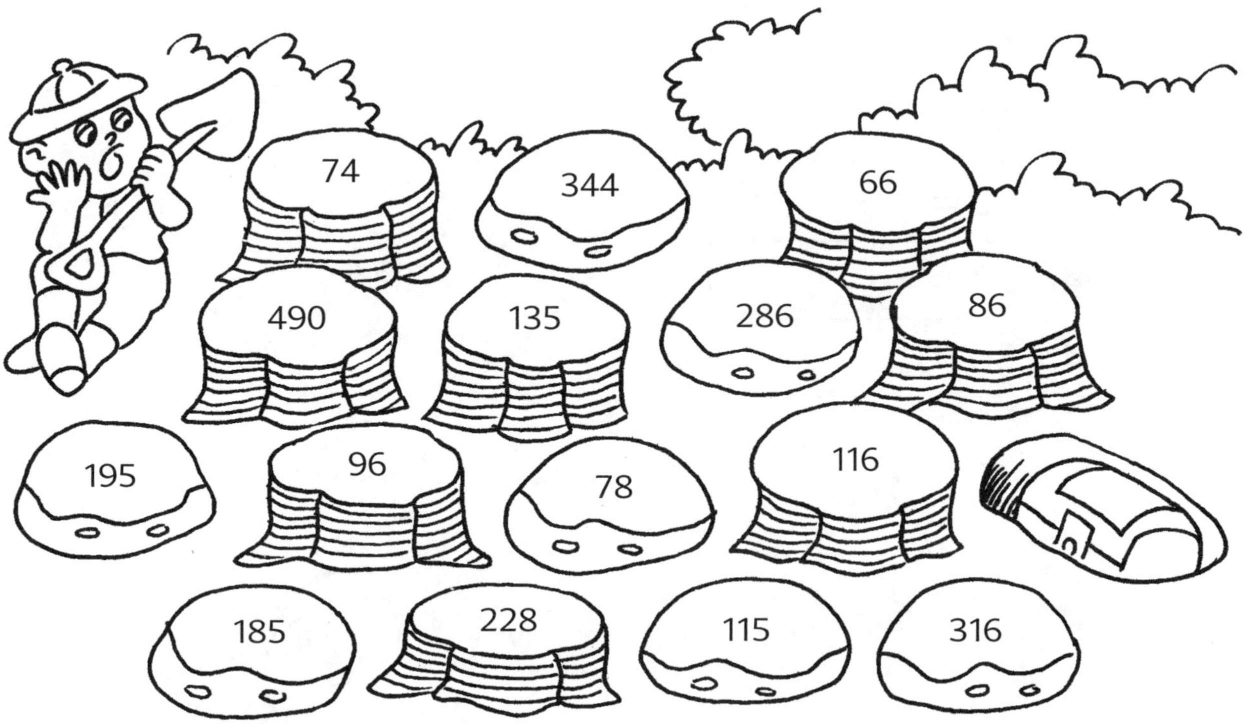

2. Find the product for each of the following. Then join the dots by following the order of the products to complete the picture.

$52 \times 2 =$
$27 \times 2 =$
$61 \times 3 =$
$24 \times 3 =$
$35 \times 4 =$
$48 \times 3 =$
$27 \times 5 =$
$4 \times 34 =$
$5 \times 26 =$
$3 \times 59 =$
$5 \times 40 =$
$5 \times 56 =$
$5 \times 80 =$
$4 \times 97 =$
$4 \times 56 =$

3. One bus can carry 46 passengers.
How many passengers can 3 buses carry?

---

4. Meilin made 5 bows.
She used 75 cm of ribbon for each bow.
How many centimetres of ribbon did she use altogether?

---

5. Raju saved $60 a month for 4 months.
How much did he save altogether?

EXERCISE 24

1. Multiply.

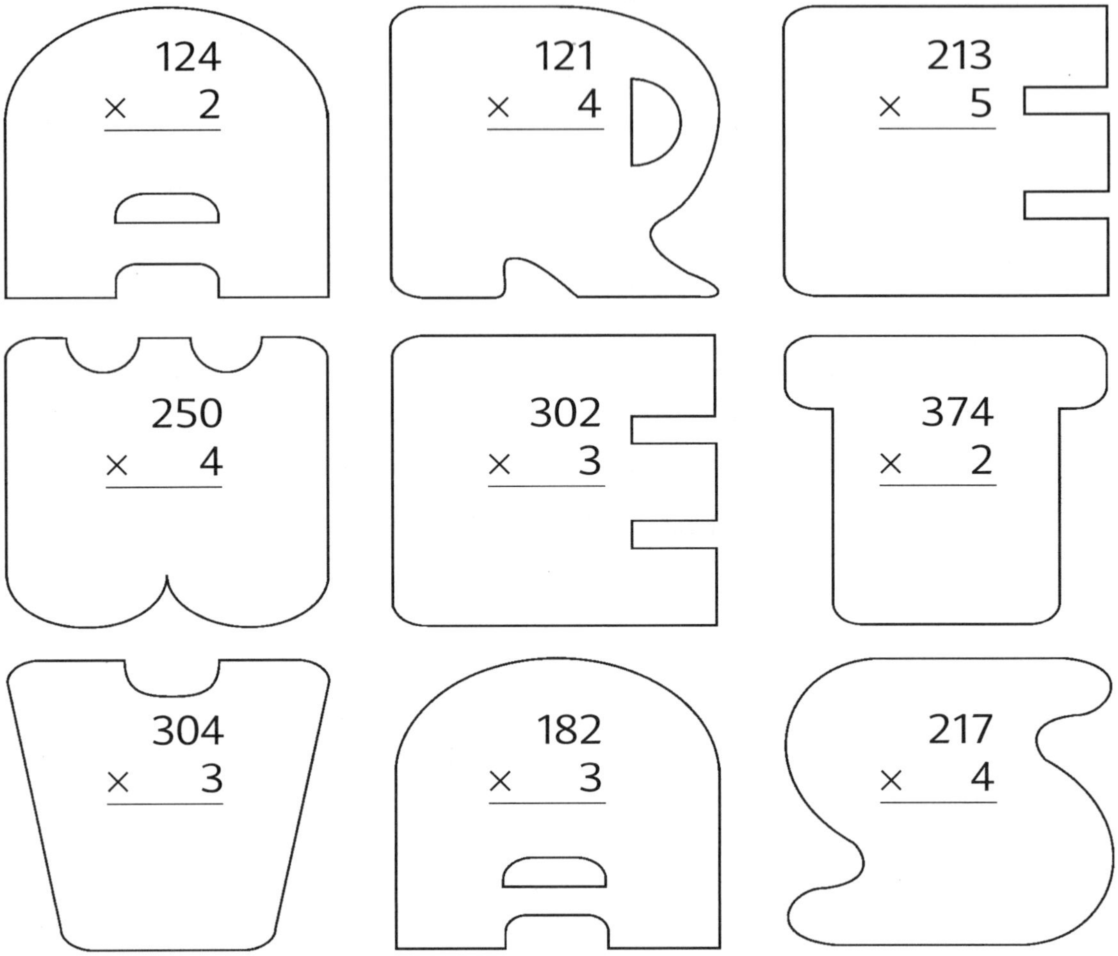

Write the letters which match the answers.
You will find a message.

	A		
868	248	912	1065

1000	546	748	906	484

2. Multiply.

3 × 145 =	308 × 5 =
4 × 264 =	495 × 2 =
8 × 500 =	280 × 5 =
2 × 163 =	700 × 3 =
5 × 214 =	837 × 4 =
4 × 135 =	369 × 3 =

Colour the spaces which contain the answers.
You will find an animal which is found in the desert.

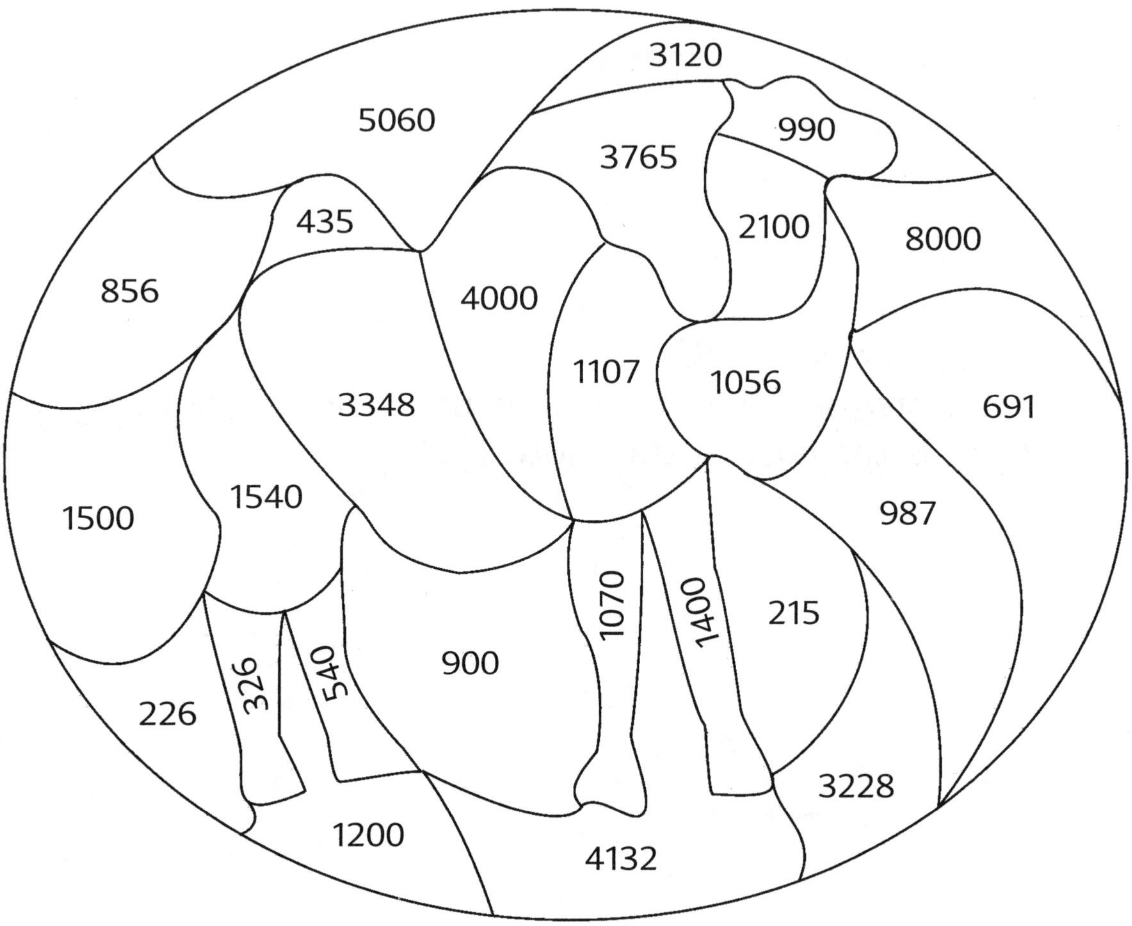

3. Samy bought 240 packets of sugar.
Each packet of sugar costs \$3.
How much did he pay altogether?

---

4. Sunshine Estate has 4 blocks of flats.
There are 104 flats in each block.
How many flats are there altogether?

---

5. A bicycle costs \$385.
A motorcycle costs 5 times as much as the bicycle.
What is the cost of the motorcycle?

EXERCISE 25

1. Divide.

What keys cannot be used to open cupboards?

Write the letters which match the answers.
You will find two of them.

M					
7 R 1	43	48	15	31 R 1	49 R 1

20	14 R 1	41 R 1	15	31 R 1	49 R 1

2. Colour the spaces which contain even numbers blue.

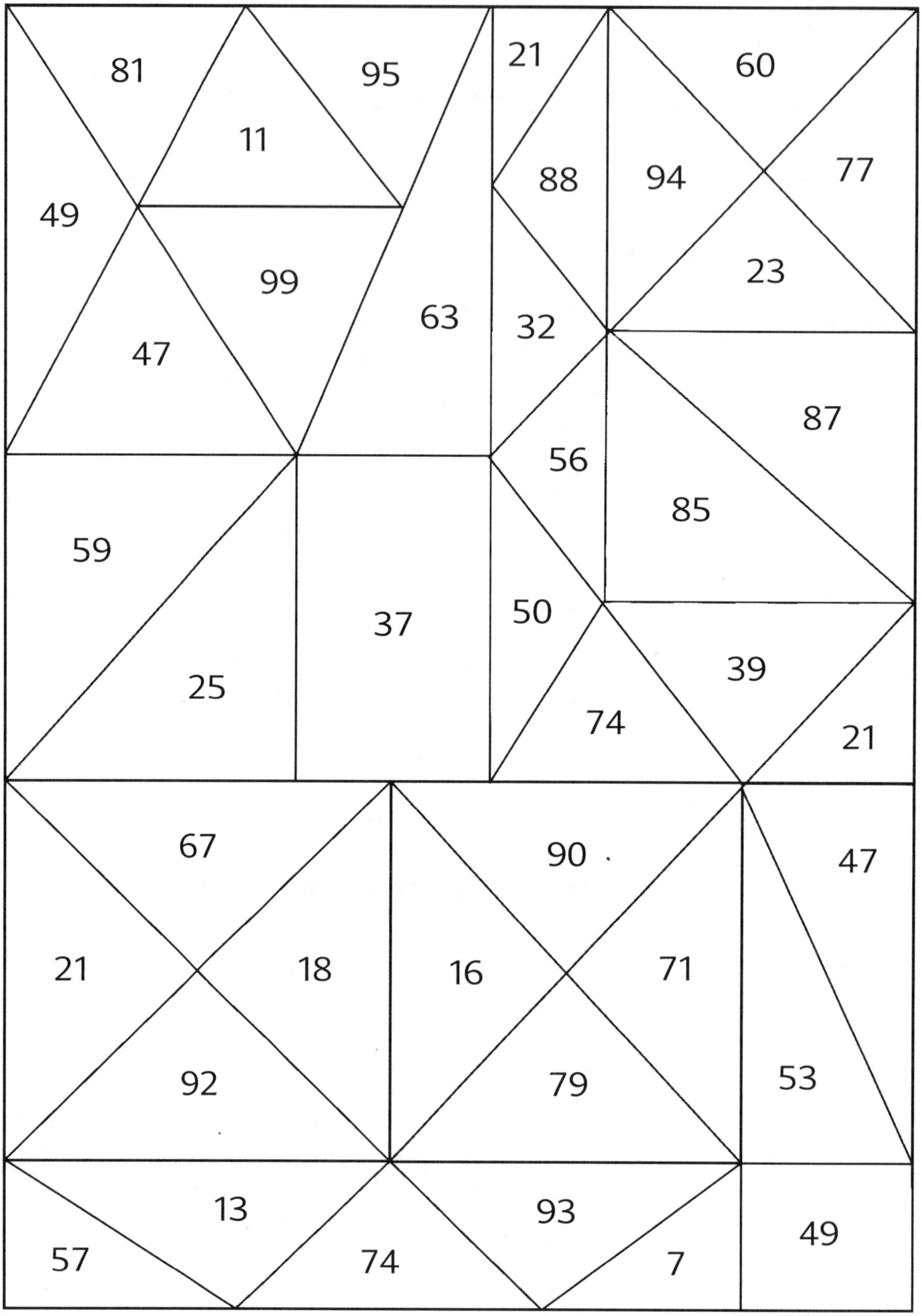

REVISION 2

1. Write the numbers.

   (a) Nine hundred and forty-two ________

   (b) Four thousand, six hundred and five ________

   (c) Three thousand and four ________

   (d) Six thousand and thirty ________

2. Write the numbers in words.

(a)	4062	
(b)	5880	

3. Write the missing numbers.

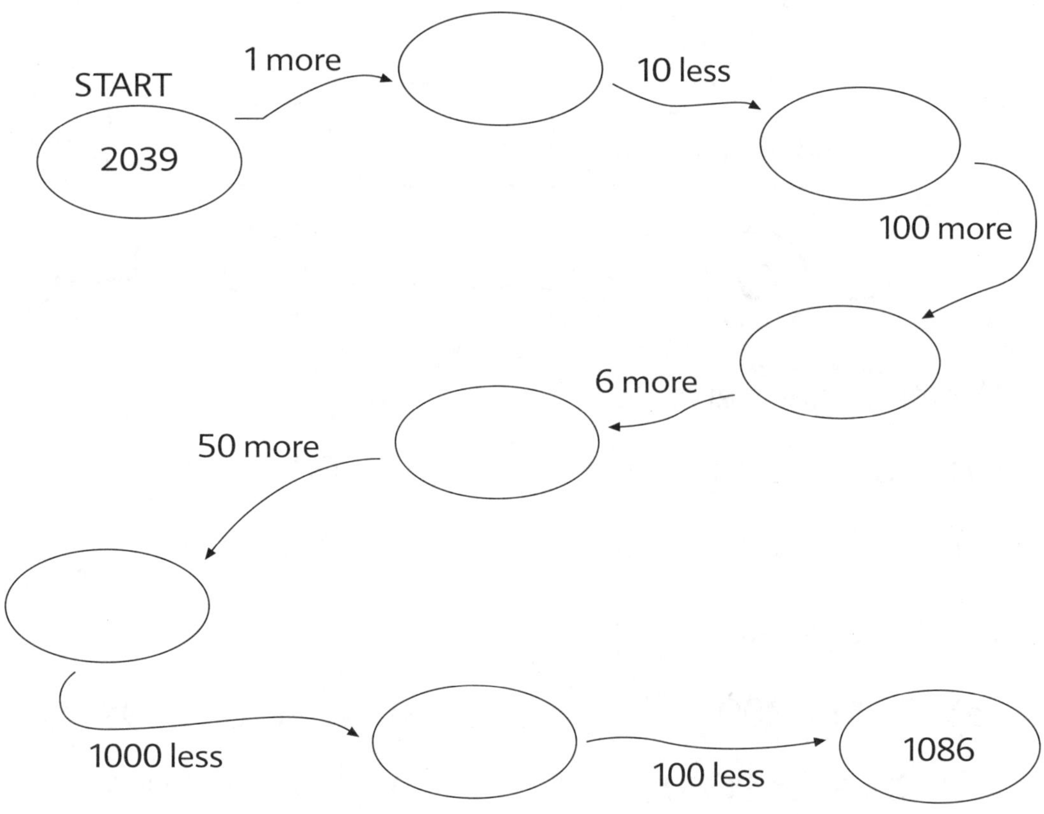

4. Write the missing numbers.

(a)

(b)

(c)

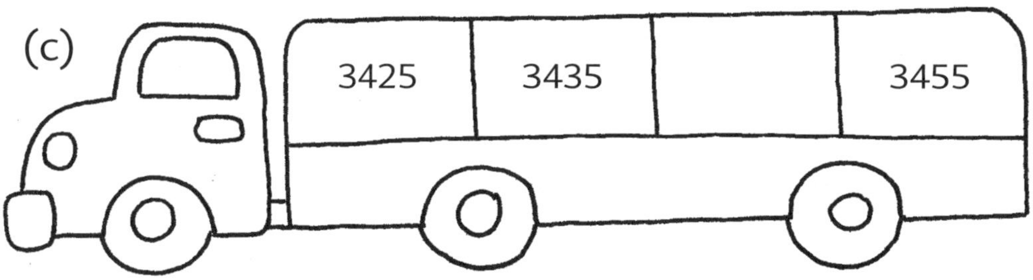

(d)

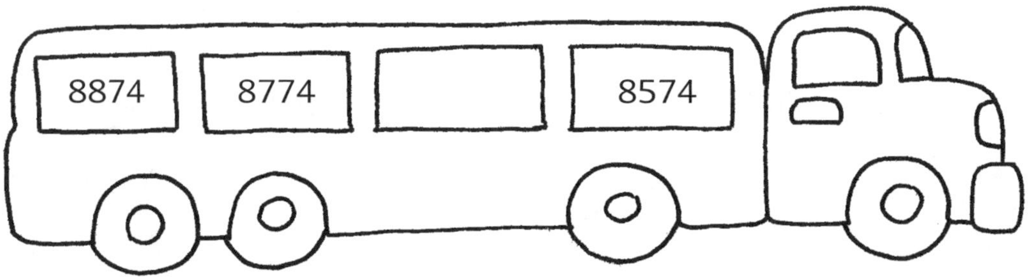

5. Which is greater?

(a) 980 or 978 ______ (b) 1008 or 1010 ______

(c) 279 or 978 ______ (d) 2109 or 2091 ______

6. Which is smaller?

(a) 312 or 309 ______ (b) 2090 or 2099 ______

(c) 9009 or 9080 ______ (d) 4779 or 5009 ______

7. There are 1407 green beads.
There are 795 fewer green beads than brown beads.
How many brown beads are there?

---

8. Mary had \$1000.
She spent \$832 and saved the rest.
How much did she save?

---

9. Lihua used 4 kg of flour to make cakes.
She used 18 eggs for each kilogram of flour.
How many eggs did she use?

10. There are 650 men and twice as many women working in a factory.
How many workers are there in the factory?

---

11. A farmer had 2000 chickens and ducks.
After selling some of them, he had 650 chickens and 520 ducks left.
How many chickens and ducks did he sell altogether?

REVISION 3

1. Complete the following tables.

(a)

×	1	2	3	4	5	6	7	8	9	10
2	2	4							18	
3			9							
4		8				24				
5								40		
10				40						

(b) Each bag of rice weighs 10 kg.

Number of bags	2	3	5	7	9	10
Total weight	20 kg					

2. Write two multiplication sentences and two division sentences.

☐ × ☐ = ☐ ☐ ÷ ☐ = ☐

☐ × ☐ = ☐ ☐ ÷ ☐ = ☐

3. Write the values of the digits in each of the following numbers.

(a) 3 7 5 1

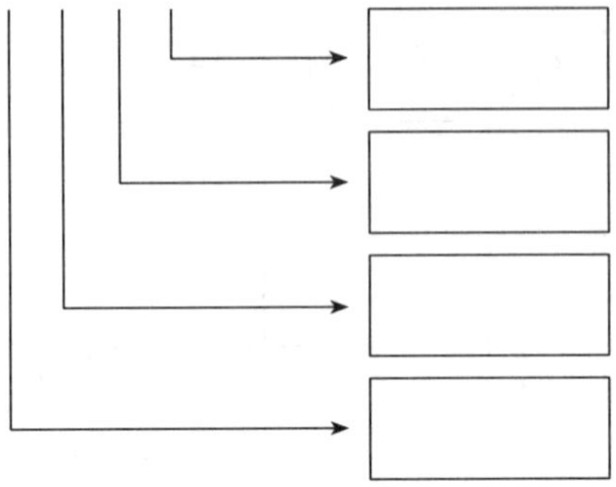

(b) 7 0 7 3

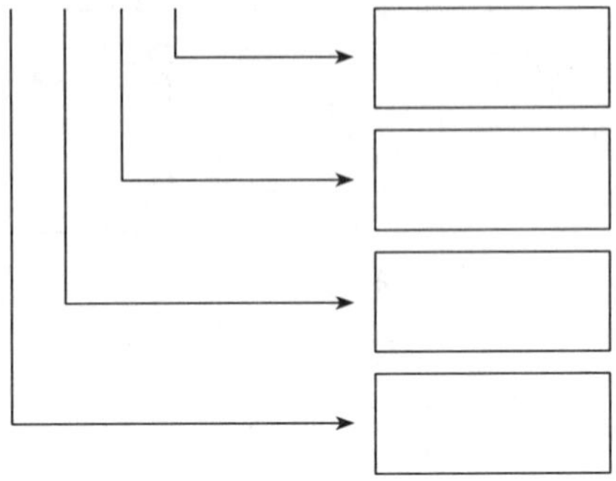

4. Fill in the blanks.

(a) 2985 is ________ less than 3000.

(b) 10 000 is 1000 more than ________.

(c) In 2546, the digit ________ is in the **hundreds place**.

(d) In 4609, the digit **0** is in the ________ place.

(e) The **difference** between 990 and 1000 is ________.

(f) When 426 is divided by 4, the **quotient** is ________ and the **remainder** is ________.

5. Write the missing numbers.

(a)

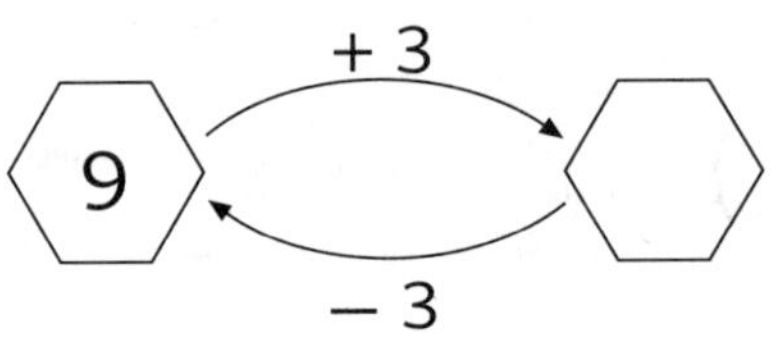

(b)

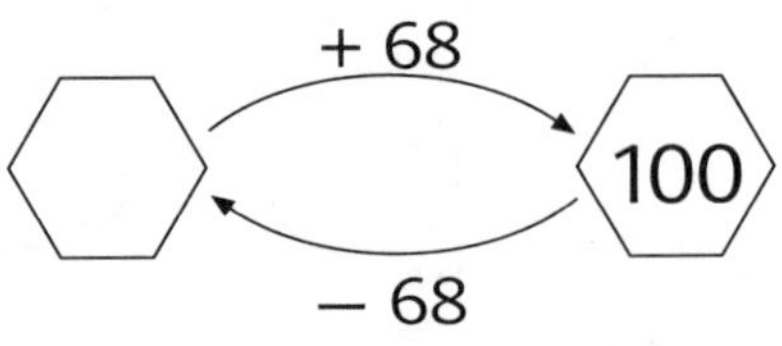

(c)

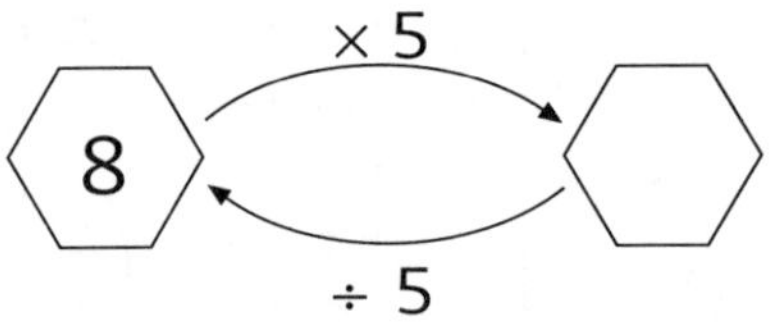

(d)

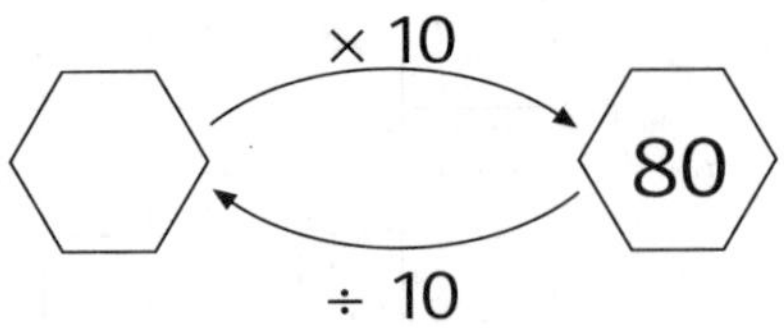

6. An album can hold 400 stickers.
   Lily has 199 stickers.
   How many more stickers does she need to fill the album?

7. Sumin bought 4 bottles of syrup to make 96 glasses of drink.
   How many glasses of drink could she make from a bottle of syrup?

8. A tape recorder costs $175.
   A typewriter costs 3 times as much as the tape recorder.
   What is the cost of the typewriter?

9. Sumin has 1200 stamps.
860 of them are Singapore stamps.
The rest are Malaysian stamps.
How many more Singapore stamps than Malaysian stamps does he have?

---

10. A computer cost $1900.
A television set was $650 cheaper than the computer.
Mr Raju bought both the computer and television set.
How much did he pay?

EXERCISE 26

1. Find the quotient and remainder.

$2\overline{)83}$

Quotient	
Remainder	

$4\overline{)65}$

Quotient	
Remainder	

$5\overline{)67}$

Quotient	
Remainder	

$3\overline{)96}$

Quotient	
Remainder	

$2\overline{)75}$

Quotient	
Remainder	

$4\overline{)78}$

Quotient	
Remainder	

$3\overline{)80}$

Quotient	
Remainder	

$5\overline{)95}$

Quotient	
Remainder	

2. Rahmat put 74 cookies equally into 3 jars.
How many cookies were there in each jar?
How many cookies were left over?

---

3. Mrs Fu sold 70 flowers.
The flowers were in bunches of 5.
How many bunches of flowers did she sell?

---

4. 96 children divided themselves into groups of 4.
How many groups were there?

EXERCISE 27

1. Divide.

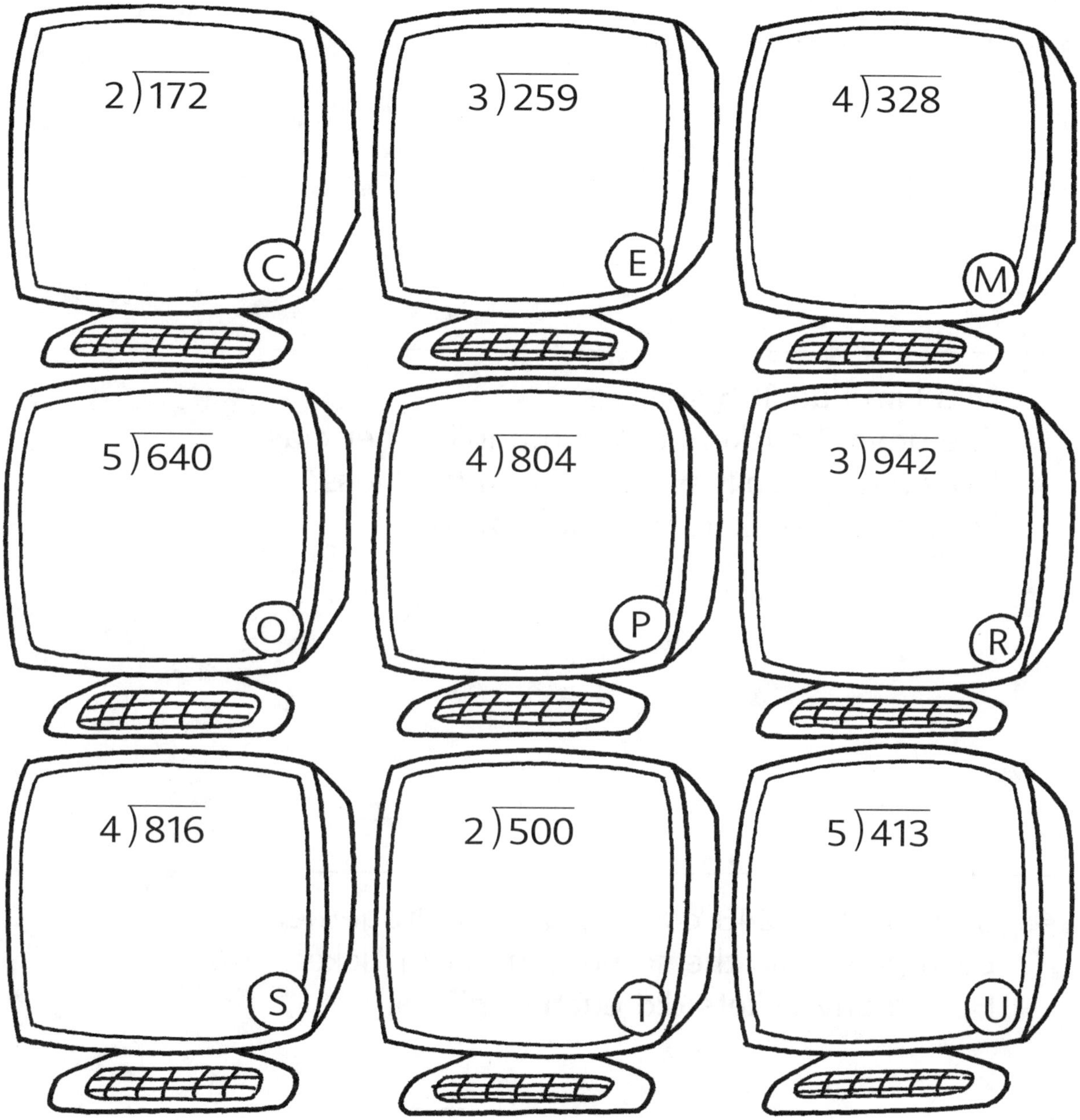

What are the machines on this page?

Write the letters which match the answers to find out.

C								
86	128	82	201	82 R 3	250	86 R 1	314	204

2. David saved $900 in 4 months.
He saved the same amount of money each month.
How much did he save a month?

---

3. Mrs Lim had 186 stickers.
She gave 5 stickers to each pupil in her class.
How many pupils were there in her class?
How many stickers were left over?

---

4. 3 pupils sold 243 concert tickets altogether.
Each pupil sold the same number of tickets.
How many tickets did each pupil sell?